Gone
Too Soon

The Life and Loss of Infants and Unborn Children

By Sherri Devashrayee Wittwer

Covenant Communications, Inc.

To my son who first let me taste the
sweetness of motherhood;

And my sons who let me feast upon it.

Published by Covenant Communications, Inc.
American Fork, Utah

Copyright © 1994 by Sherri Devashrayee Wittwer
All rights reserved

Printed in the United States of America
First Printing: January 1994

01 00 99 98 97 96 95   10 9 8 7 6 5 4 3 2

Library of Congress Cataloging-in-Publication Data

Wittwer, Sherri Devashrayee, 1967-

      Gone too soon: the life and loss of infants and unborn children/ Sherri Devashrayee Wittwer

      p. cm.

Includes bibliographical references.

ISBN 1-55503-655-4 : $7.95

1. Death--Religious aspects--Mormon Church. 2. Infants (Newborn)--Death--Religious aspects--Mormon
Church. 3. Fetal death--Religious aspects--Mormon Church. 4. Bereavement--Religious aspects--Mormon
Church. 5. Church of Jesus Christ of Latter-day Saints--Doctrines. 6. Consolation. I. Title.

BX8643.D4w58   1994

248.8'6--dc20   93-48938

                                       CIP

Contents

Acknowledgments

I would like to express my sincerest gratitude to the many men and women who, having experienced a loss, were so willing to talk to me. They helped me to find the scope of this book as they shared their most precious, sacred thoughts and experiences. These couples have demonstrated to me the meaning of true strength and courage, and I pray that they may find peace and happiness.

Thanks also to my reviewers who, despite very busy schedules, were able and willing to offer their invaluable insights. I am especially grateful to Dr. L. Kimball Lloyd, Judy Jenkins, Laurel Osborn, and John W. Wittwer.

Special thanks to my good friend and "co-conspirator," Susan Jensen. It is through her confidence, support, and inspired friendship that this project has come to fruition.

I would also like to thank my mother, Kirsten Devashrayee. She is my "buddy," confidant, and mentor. She is the supreme example of motherhood. There were many days that, without her love, I would have never have survived.

Finally, I would like to express my gratitude to my husband, David. He has allowed me to lean on his strength, even when he has felt weak; to learn from his wisdom, even when answers have eluded him; and to flourish in his love—the rarest and purest love I have ever known. I am forever grateful and forever blessed for the way he loves me.

Preface

Through a Glass, Darkly

For now we see through a glass, darkly; but then face to face: now I know in part; but then shall I know even as also I am known. —1 Corinthians 13:12

"It's not a baby, you know," the man said. "It's just a blob of cells—of that protoplasm stuff." I had heard the comment time and time again and had felt its familiar sting. But this time, the sting felt more like a blow. Only weeks earlier, I had miscarried a little boy after nearly fourteen weeks of pregnancy. The experience had shattered my heart, my soul, my entire being into millions of tiny pieces. I was left with the tedious task of shaping those pieces back to their original, whole form. Yet I knew that the task was impossible. Some of those pieces were so drastically altered that they would never fit together again; others were permanently lost. And now this, adding insult to injury—to have to deal with the cynics and disbelievers who told me that my baby was in actuality some bizarre and hallucinatory figment of my imagination. That to lose a baby was no more traumatic than losing an appendix or a wisdom tooth. To be told by those same weavers of myths and half-truths that I "hadn't even had time to bond with the fetus yet."

I wish those same disbelievers could have peeked, only for a moment, into the darkest corner of my life where I sat on the floor after feeling my little son slip out of my body to a certain death. The incredible horror and agony of those moments were simply beyond description. And yet, in the midst of tragedy and despair, I was able to witness the miracle of God's creation. As I held my son in the palm of my hand, I was astonished at the perfection of his tiny form. I saw a beautiful face already bearing resemblance to family members, complete with eyes, tiny ears, a little mouth and nose. I will never forget how I looked with wonder at tiny, perfect fingers and toes. With the exception of time, my son had everything he needed to be a normal, healthy baby. For some inexplicable reason, my inhospitable body had refused to allow for that necessary time.

So who or what was this—this "fetus" so often referred to as a blob, a mass of cells, an organ? Why did he make this uncertain and transitory passage through my life? Did he have a part in God's plan, in our eternal plan, or was he a mere mishap, a fluke, completely expendable and replaceable? And what of the millions of other babies not only tragically miscarried or stillborn, but also those legally and deliberately aborted?

And finally, how do I put the pieces of my life back together into a replica of its once whole form? Is it possible to not merely reproduce that form, but somehow to actually improve upon it?

We look at these questions through what the scriptures call "a glass, darkly," for we have no perfect knowledge of the life and mission of the unborn baby. Indeed, its life is shrouded in ambiguity, misrepresentation, and, too often, indifference. Concrete answers are not currently available to us.

However, through the gospel of Jesus Christ, science, and the testimonies of women who have experienced the loss of a baby through miscarriage, ectopic pregnancy, stillbirth, or infant death, some explanations and discoveries can be found. For, whether a woman successfully gives birth to a baby, loses a baby due to complications of the pregnancy, or even aborts her unborn child only later to recognize the horror that accompanies such a loss, one thing is certain: Once a woman carries a baby, her life will be altered forever.

There are irrefutable truths that, for now, we can embrace and in which we can find peace. As for myself, I believe that someday the enigmatic glass will be removed, and I will know the complete purpose of my baby's life and his brief passage in and out of mine. For now, "I know in part; but then shall I know even as also I am known." And someday, I will know "face to face."

ONE

The Life of the Unborn Baby

I will praise thee; for I am fearfully and wonderfully made: marvellous are thy works; and that my soul knoweth right well. My substance was not hid from thee, when I was made in secret.—Psalms 139:14-15

In the Latter-day Saint culture, family is all-important. We realize that our most esteemed role is that of mothers and fathers as we receive and then train Heavenly Father's special spirits to return to him someday. One of the most important commandments is to "multiply and replenish the earth," and the ultimate goal is an eternal family. Perhaps this emphasis on family and on bringing these spirits to earth contributes to the trauma when complications with childbearing arise. We *know* that these babies are important. Therefore, it can be frustrating when we feel that we are trying to follow the Lord's commandments and still no healthy babies come. However, even though these babies are not allowed to live on this earth outside of their mothers' bodies, they are significant human beings. Even physically, there is more to these babies--even the tiniest ones--than most people realize.

For many couples, one of the most difficult challenges they face is the refusal of society to acknowledge that the loss of an unborn baby is the loss of a unique individual. Such an attitude is not surprising when the question "When does life begin?" remains unanswered. Scientists, doctors, philosophers, and theologians continue to debate the intricacies of the issue, with a consensus seeming unlikely.

However, modern technology gives remarkable insight into the pre-birth activity of this tiny baby. Today, the physician and even the expectant parents are able to peek into the womb and witness their baby in action. Hence, physicians are able to diagnose (and in many cases treat) potential problems with the baby or the pregnancy in general. With increased knowledge, parents are able to more easily bond with their child long before its actual birth. This bonding opportunity can be powerful, but it can also make the pain much more severe if the baby dies. Nonetheless, science is continually learning more about these tiny people and their development, capabilities, and even personality. The miracle of a baby's creation, however, begins long before even science can detect.

Just One Cell

Upon fertilization, when the ovum and the sperm unite, a single cell emerges. Now, a lone cell may not sound particularly interesting, but take into account its unique properties:[1]

- The cell is now either male or female.
- The genetic coding responsible for the color of the hair, eyes, skin, facial features, body type, and certain qualities of personality and intelligence have already been determined.
- The cell is complete. Nothing but nutrition and oxygen will be added from this time forth.
- The new being is programmed from within. It moves forward in a self-controlled, ongoing process of growth.
- This being is responsible for its own growth, development, and replacement of its own dying cells.
- This cell has never before existed in the history of the

world, and never will another individual exactly like it exist.

- It is this cell that continues to grow and create the changes in its mother's body to prepare for the pregnancy and eventual delivery. This baby will even determine its own birthday.

Fetal Development

To completely understand the miracle of human creation, it is necessary to know something about the development of the baby while in the womb.

After fertilization takes place, the developing baby, through its own nurturing placenta, comes to rest within the uterus. The baby intends to stay in this "home" for the next 260 to 270 days. The fertilized ovum is now known in scientific terms as an *embryo*. As it develops, it creates its own life support system. This includes its own "space capsule" (the amniotic sac), its own "lifeline" (the umbilical cord), and its own "root system" (the placenta). These all belong to the baby, not the mother, as they are developed from the original fertilized ovum. The mother and baby are separate individuals from the time of fertilization, but the baby is dependent upon the mother to provide the nourishment it will receive.

It is interesting to note that major developments in the unborn baby take place very early in the pregnancy. At 18 days following conception, the heart begins to beat, and by 21 days it is pumping blood (which may be a different type than the mother's) through a closed circulatory system.

At 40 days, electrical waves from the baby's brain can be recorded on an electroencephalogram (EEG), thus indicating brain function.

In the sixth and seventh weeks, the developing baby first moves. This is the stage during which most women suspect and discover that they are pregnant.

By eight weeks, all of the baby's body systems are present. Perhaps the most dramatic account of the baby at this stage of development is that given by Dr. P. E. Rockwell:

> Eleven years ago, while giving an anesthetic for a ruptured tubal pregnancy (at two months), I was handed what I believed to be the smallest human being ever seen. The embryo sac was intact and transparent. Within the sac was a tiny (one-third inch) human male swimming extremely vigorously in the amniotic fluid, while attached to the wall by the umbilical cord. This tiny human was perfectly developed with long, tapering fingers, feet, and toes. It was almost transparent as regards the skin, and the delicate arteries and veins were prominent to the ends of the fingers.
>
> The baby was extremely alive and swam about the sac with a natural swimmer's stroke. This tiny human did not look at all like the photos and drawings of 'embryos' which I have seen, nor did it look like the few embryos I have been able to observe since then, obviously because this one was alive.
>
> When the sac was opened, the tiny human immediately lost its life and took on the appearance of what is accepted as the appearance of an embryo at this stage (blunt extremities, etc.).

As the pregnancy progresses and the baby approaches nine to ten weeks, it squints, swallows, moves its tongue, and if you stroke its palm, will make a tight fist. It will bend its fingers around an object in the palm of its hand. It is also "not uncommon radiologically, to find fetuses sucking fingers, thumbs, and toes, and thumbsucking has been photographed in the nine-week abortus."

By 11 to 12 weeks (three months), the baby is breathing in amniotic fluid, and at this point all of the body systems are working.

After the first few weeks of rapid growth of the major organs, later months show the growth and development of the "details" on the baby.

At four and one-half months, a very bright light on a woman's abdomen will cause the baby to slowly move its hand to a position shielding the eyes. Loud music will cause the baby to cover its ears.

In the fifth month (if not before), the mother feels the baby's movements as it becomes larger and stronger. The baby can sleep and wake and hiccup.

During the sixth month, the baby responds to its mother's heartbeat and recognizes her voice.

Dr. A. Liley, often referred to as the father of Fetology, states this about the unborn baby:

> We know that he moves with a delightful easy grace in his buoyant world, that fetal comfort determines fetal position. He is responsive to pain and touch and cold and sound and light. He drinks his amniotic fluid, more if it is artificially sweetened, less if it is given an unpleasant taste. He gets hiccups and sucks his thumb. He wakes and sleeps. He gets bored with repetitive signals but can be taught to be alerted by a first signal for a second different one. And, finally, he determines his birthday, for unquestionably, the onset of labour is a unilateral decision of the foetus.
>
> This, then, is the foetus we know and, indeed, we each once were. This is the foetus we look after in modern obstetrics, the same baby we are caring for before and after birth, who before birth can be ill and need diagnosis and treatment just like any other patient.

The Personality of the Unborn Baby
Physically, the unborn baby takes on human characteristics. But does the unborn baby have a personality? Ask any expectant mother, and she will tell you that her baby's

personality is very apparent by the baby's level of activity. Furthermore, some mothers claim that each baby they carried behaved differently and that the baby's behavior in the womb mirrored the baby's behavior after birth—even into adulthood.

Some doctors, too, believe that a baby's personality is apparent even in the womb. Dr. Liley states:

> Distinctions can be observed between foetuses before birth, not only in their physical appearance, in their physiological appearance, but also in their activity states, their responses to external stimuli. In other words, it is not just appearance, but also, behaviour, by which they can be distinguished.

Indications that an unborn baby actually has a personality and is affected emotionally by external stimuli have been described in this way:

> We now know that the unborn child is an aware, reacting human being who from the sixth month on (and perhaps earlier) leads an active, emotional life.
> The fetus can, on a primitive level, even learn in utero.
> Whether he ultimately sees himself and, hence, acts as a sad or happy, aggressive or meek, secure or anxiety-ridden person depends, in part, on the messages he gets about himself in the womb.

Finally, Dr. W. Freud observed 10,000 ultrasound visualizations and reported, "It looks as if the fetus has a lot of intentionality." He further described witnessing unborn twins fighting.

The wonders of modern technology have afforded us the ability to make discoveries about the unborn baby that we never dreamed were possible. Today, premature babies are being saved at an age that just a few years ago would have been considered "late miscarriages." Surgery is being performed on the unborn baby while still in the womb. Parents are able to bond with babies early in the pregnancy as they witness the baby's activity on ultrasound. And the question, "When does life begin?" becomes increasingly complicated.

However, one fact becomes clear: The life of the unborn baby is truly significant, and when a baby is lost, it is indeed the loss of something—someone—very special.

Notes

1. Information on fetal development quoted from Dr. and Mrs. J. C. Willke, *Abortion Questions and Answers* (Cincinnati: Hayes Publishing Co., 1985); and from "Abortion: Death before Life" (pamphlet), National Right to Life Educational Trust fund.

TWO

To Lose a Baby

Before I formed thee in the belly I knew thee; and before thou camest forth out of the womb I sanctified thee. —Jeremiah 1:5

The "miracle of birth": it's a phrase that is tossed about lightly, perhaps with an air of frivolity. Expectant parents are told that "women have babies every day," that pregnancy is nothing but a "normal" condition, and that there is "nothing to worry about." Yet, somewhere amidst the quiet regularity of pregnancy and birth, there is often an element of risk. That risk can lead to some of the worst pain imaginable—the loss of a child. Indeed, to many women and men whose experiences with this "miracle" have yielded disappointment and heartache, the birth process is regarded with nothing less than reverence and deep appreciation. And giving birth to a healthy baby is nothing, if not truly miraculous.

Many times the dreams, hopes, and plans of a new life begin with the knowledge that there is, indeed, a baby on the way. But these dreams that once brought so much joy can be shattered in moments by a miscarriage, ectopic pregnancy, stillbirth, or by having an infant that lives only for a short while. Regardless of how the babies die and their differing circumstances, the one stark similarity in each case is the deep sorrow and pain resulting from such a loss.

Nothing better illustrates the impact of the loss of a baby than to see a mother who, having lost a baby through stillbirth fifty years ago, wells up with emotion as she talks about her baby's life. This woman has nine living children, forty-one grandchildren, and five great-grandchildren; yet the pain she felt those many years ago is still very much in evidence. Losing a baby is indeed a life-changing event, much as is giving birth to a healthy baby.

Even though the pain may be intense and despair may seem inevitable, those who lose babies need not be subject to a life of hopelessness. Through the gospel of Jesus Christ, a loving support system, and a few techniques to help deal with grief, the pain can be managed and eased.

Today, we are fortunate that health-care professionals are increasingly more sensitive to this tender loss. No longer must grieving mothers suffer in the maternity ward, hearing the cries of other healthy babies. No longer are stillborn babies quickly whisked from the sight of the mother following delivery. No longer are all choices and decisions regarding burial kept from the grieving parents. And finally, parents are increasingly given permission to grieve, and are given tools to help them deal with their great loss.

Through the use of these tools, parents are discovering that what seems unbearable pain today will eventually subside. Although these babies are never forgotten, time heals. As one woman stated, "I used to find myself consumed with grief, and then one day I noticed that it had been an hour since I had thought about the baby; and then another day I noticed that an afternoon had passed without my thinking of him. Before I knew it, hours turned into days, and I knew that I was learning to deal with my loss. Now I can concentrate on the simple beauty of his life and the good that has come out of that experience."

To understand the grief and healing process that occurs

when a parent experiences a loss, we need to understand the different ways in which babies' lives end and the unique problems that can accompany each situation.

Miscarriage

Laura, a mother of four, describes the miscarriage of her second baby: "I had problems with the pregnancy at the very beginning. The doctor told me to rest and keep my feet up. I followed his orders, but at seven weeks, I lost the baby anyway. Since I wasn't very far along, no one seemed concerned about my loss. In fact, everyone who knew about it doubted that I was even pregnant. Even my husband picked me up from the doctor, dropped me off at home and went back to work. No one even considered the fact that I might be hurting."

Laura's story is not unusual. Often the pain accompanying the loss of a baby is dismissed, especially if the pregnancy was brief. This lack of concern for the woman's feelings can leave her frustrated and feeling abnormal.

Writer Susan Erling further elaborates on the emotions that can accompany a miscarriage:

Just Those Few Weeks
(A Poem on Miscarriage)

For those few weeks—
I had you to myself.
And that seems too short a time
to be changed so profoundly.

In those few weeks—
I came to know you . . .
and to love you.
You came to trust me with your life.
Oh, what a life I had planned for you!

Just those few weeks—
When I lost you.
I lost a lifetime of hopes,
plans, dreams, and aspirations. . .
A slice of my future simply vanished overnight.

Just those few weeks—
It wasn't enough to convince others
how special and important you were.
How odd, a truly unique person has recently died
and no one is mourning the passing.

Just a mere few weeks—
And no "normal" person would cry all night
over a tiny, unfinished baby,
or get depressed and withdraw day after endless day.
No one would, so why am I?

You were those few weeks my little one
you darted in and out of my life too quickly.
But it seems that's all the time you needed
to make my life so much richer
and give me a small glimpse of eternity.

Copyright, Susan Erling
Excerpted with permission from *Rainbow After A Storm*

Medical Facts

Miscarriage can be very frustrating because of the lack of information regarding its cause. As many as one in every three pregnancies ends in miscarriage.[1] However, the reasons for miscarriage are vague and varied. The majority of miscarriages occur because of chromosomal abnormalities which are incompatible with normal development and life. Another relatively common cause, also due to a chromosomal problem, is a "blighted ovum." In this case, the fertilized egg has formed the sac in which the embryo normally develops, but no baby has formed inside. Other causes of miscarriage include hormone deficiencies, immunological causes in which the mother's body rejects the baby as "foreign matter," and in the second trimester, an "incompetent cervix" in which the cervix is too weak to keep the baby in.[2] Doctors are also beginning to focus on the role that dangerous microorganisms and other infections can play in causing miscarriages.[3]

When a woman suffers just one miscarriage, doctors typically ascribe it to a "random genetic error." Indeed, in the vast majority of women who have experienced a miscarriage, doctors never find a cause. And even after several miscarriages, the odds are good that a woman will carry her next pregnancy to term without treatment.[4]

Ectopic Pregnancy

June, a mother of three, describes her experience with an ectopic pregnancy: "My husband and I were so excited to discover that we were expecting our second child, and we started making the usual preparations for the baby. Then I started experiencing severe pain in my lower right side. When I went to my doctor, it was discovered that the baby had implanted in my fallopian tube. Surgery was immediately performed, and I found out that I had lost a little boy. I know this sounds crazy, but I felt as if I had had an abortion. To consent to the surgery that would kill my baby was the hardest thing I had to do. I know that I could have died as well, but still I couldn't shake the feeling that I was purposefully killing him."

Medical Facts

Ectopic pregnancy occurs when the fertilized ovum implants itself outside of the uterus, usually in a fallopian tube. An ectopic pregnancy usually aborts or ruptures in the tube within three months because the baby cannot receive the proper nourishment necessary to grow or expand to its necessary proportions. An ectopic pregnancy can be life-threatening to the mother, and therefore it is necessary to remove the baby as early in the pregnancy as possible. The structure harboring the baby must generally be removed as well, because of the damage incurred by the pregnancy.

Stillbirth

Jean, whose second baby daughter was stillborn, shares her experience: "I had three miscarriages before I got pregnant with this baby, all of which were very difficult. Therefore, when we got past a certain point in this pregnancy, we thought we had made it. We had no reason to believe that there was any kind of problem. I had carried the baby full-term when I went in for my routine pre-natal check-up. I will never forget the doctor searching for the baby's heartbeat, but being unable to find it. Still, I just hoped that there was a simple solution to it all, and that the baby would be fine. But a few hours later, labor was induced and after a difficult labor and delivery, our baby girl was born dead. We were devastated. We did feel fortunate, however, that we were able to hold our baby, take pictures and keep her in my room with us for awhile. One of the hardest things, though, is that we still don't know why our baby died. To have this baby complete and perfect and to not know why she died is so hard."

One insightful writer elaborates on the emotions associated with a stillbirth:

Stillborn

I carried you in hope,
the long nine months of my term,
remembered that close hour when we made you,
often felt you kick and move
as slowly you grew within me,
wondered what you would look like
when your wet head emerged,
girl or boy, and at that glad moment

I should hear your birth cry,
and I welcoming you
with all you needed of warmth and food;
we had a home waiting for you.

After my strong labourings,
sweat cold on my limbs,
my small cries merging with the summer air
you came. You did not cry.
You did not breathe.
We had not expected this;
It seems your birth had no meaning,
or had you rejected us?

They will say that you did not live,
register you as stillborn.
But you lived for me all that time
in the dark chamber of my womb,
and when I think of you now,
perfect in your little death,
I know that you are born still,
I shall carry you with me forever,
my child, you were always mine,
you are mine now.

Death and life are the same mysteries.

Leonard Clark in *Education and Counseling for Childbirth*
by Sheila Kitzinger, Schnocken Books, 1979

Medical Facts

Although the causes for stillbirths are very often unknown, a good number occur because of what are often referred to as "cord accidents." Sometimes the umbilical cord can get wrapped around the baby's neck or another part of the body, a knot can occur in the cord, or the cord is compressed, causing the baby's death. Other times there is a defect in the cord, membranes, or in the placenta that causes the death. Still other causes include maternal diabetes, post-term pregnancies, and toxemia, which render the placenta or baby incapable of sustaining life. A large number of parents, however, live with the frustration of never having discovered the reason for their baby's death.

Infant Death

Michelle was sent to bed after she went into premature labor at six months. "I spent all of my energies on the baby and kept thinking about how life would be after the baby came. I never dreamed that things would end the way they did." Michelle carried the baby just short of full-term and delivered what was announced to be a healthy baby girl. "We were so happy that we had made it after worrying so much. They took me to my room to recover; but just a few hours later, my husband came in to tell me that our baby had been diagnosed with Group-B Strep and was rushed to another hospital. Still, we believed that she would pull through—we simply hadn't prepared for anything else. But on the third day of her life, the doctors told us there was no hope and they took her off life support. We got to hold her for those last few moments and take pictures of her; and then she was gone."

Medical Facts

Unfortunately, there are many different causes of infant death, and many different circumstances surrounding these deaths which deserve special mention.

Statistics show that the primary cause of infant death is complications resulting from a premature birth. Many couples can relate to the unique pain of delivering a baby early, only to watch the baby be sustained by life support and other special measures. These parents speak of their incredible "roller coaster" of emotions as the baby has good and bad days. Some parents' lives are lived out in hospitals for weeks and months as they offer these tiny babies their needed love and support. Sadly, even though many babies are sustained for long periods of time giving the family hope, they still die after fighting an uphill battle. Much is being done in the medical community to develop better technology for the care of these little ones.

Other causes of infant death are congenital anomalies, especially heart defects, respiratory problems, complications due to problems with the cord, placenta and membranes, infection, and other maternal complications. Some parents know of these complications before the baby's birth, and others are completely taken by surprise after the baby's birth. Some babies, again, are sustained in the hospital until their death, and other babies are allowed to be taken home. Many parents can relate to the experience of taking a sick baby home to die. They try to enjoy their babies for the time that they have, but they must deal with the stress of caring for a baby with special needs, knowing that the baby cannot live for long.

With older babies, accidental death becomes an issue. In babies between the ages of two and four months, the leading cause of death is Sudden Infant Death Syndrome, otherwise known as SIDS or "crib death." In this syndrome, the babies are usually discovered after having passed away in their sleep. This is a particularly devastating death for the parents to deal with, because prior to death, the baby appears to be healthy and they have no reason to suspect that anything is wrong. These parents cope with the special pain of having welcomed the baby into their family, only to have it die unexpectedly. Their burden of guilt is enormous, as they feel that they should have suspected something and should have been able to prevent the death. But this kind of guilt is completely unfounded. While there are many theories as to why such deaths occur, there are no known cures or absolute preventative measures that will ensure the safety of infants.

Society's Contribution to the Pain

Being aware that the loss of a baby is not uncommon, and even having an understanding of the medical reasons behind the loss, does not relieve the emotional pain. The loss of a baby at any stage of development yields an unusual sort of grief because, for the most part, society refuses to acknowledge the pain that comes from a failed pregnancy. In fact, it holds that unborn babies have no legal rights and can even be legally destroyed. The general attitude toward miscarriage or ectopic pregnancy is that because the baby was perhaps never held or seen, or because the woman carried it for only a few weeks, the parents didn't really have enough time to truly "know" that baby, and the loss is therefore dismissed. Few people understand that the fact that the parents never have an opportunity to know their child better *is* the tragedy.

It is cruel to assume that if the child has not breathed outside of the womb, then the loss is insignificant. Similarly, to judge the gravity of the loss by weeks of gestation is unfair. However, the fact remains that while parents who lose a newborn are given some time to grieve, parents who have stillborn babies are given even less time to grieve, and parents who lose a baby through miscarriage or ectopic pregnancy are given very little time, if any, to recover emotionally.

Virtually every woman who has lost a baby has had at least one experience which illustrates society's lack of compassion for women facing this challenge. One woman explains her experience with the callousness of others after she lost her baby three months into the pregnancy. While discussing her miscarriage with a coworker, she was shocked when he remarked, "Well at least you didn't bond with the baby yet." As she reflects, "If I hadn't bonded with my child by that point, why was my life falling apart? To have people minimize your pain when it fills the whole world is the hardest thing I had to go through." Another woman observes, "People think losing a baby involves a little physical pain and then in a few days you should be back on your feet, moving on with your life, and trying to get pregnant again." And another comments, "I got so tired of people hearing of our baby's death and dismissing our pain with comments like, 'Well, I knew someone who lost a baby at twenty weeks, or thirty weeks, or full-term.'"

The need to make arbitrary classifications of loss is a curious creation of our "disposable" society. Rather than accepting any loss as valid and genuine, society tends to take a person's loss and minimize it by comparing it to other tragedies. The absurdity in society's assessment of loss is clear; after all, when *is* a good time to lose a loved one?

The only people who can determine the gravity of a baby's death are the grieving parents. While some parents may grieve very deeply for long periods of time, others may be able to recover relatively quickly. Either reaction to such a loss is completely normal. But why do some women find the loss of a baby to be so traumatic in the first place?

Jane Forsyth, a therapist who has experienced a miscarriage, explains that miscarriage is perhaps the only phenomenon in which an individual experiences the death of another literally inside of her and attached to her. Hence the special significance of the expression, "I feel like something inside me has died." To be so closely attached, first to life and then to death, brings a woman's own mortality to consciousness, increasing her sense of vulnerability and forcing her to confront issues of control, depression, guilt, fear, and anger.[5] This assessment can be readily applied to ectopic pregnancy, stillbirth, and infant death as well.

It is this "something" inside the woman that awakens her maternal instinct and her primal longing to protect, nurture, and love her offspring. Contrary to the beliefs of some, the parent-infant bonding process can begin long before birth. Indeed, the bonding between mother and unborn baby invokes some of the most powerful and significant emotions that a woman can experience. In his novel *The Grapes of Wrath*, John Steinbeck beautifully describes his character Rose of Sharon and the bond she shares with her unborn baby:

> . . . her whole body had become demure
> and serious. Her whole thought and action
> were directed inward on the baby. She balanced
> on her toes now, for the baby's sake. And the
> world was pregnant to her; she thought only in
> terms of reproduction and motherhood.[6]

When a woman becomes pregnant, she redirects her life completely. First, she concentrates on the child within her body and its growth, strength and well-being. This includes good nutrition, prenatal visits to the doctor, etc. Then the woman concentrates on restructuring her environment to prepare for the child—preparing the nursery, the baby's clothing, etc. When a woman bonds with and prepares for the child, but returns home from the hospital or doctor's office with empty arms, the result can be devastating. To have that child so close and then to have it abruptly taken away might well be viewed as one of the cruelest occurrences in nature.

Babies symbolize life, innocence, and unconditional love. To associate a baby with death goes completely against all expectations. Babies, the beginning of life, should not enter the world at what is seemingly the end. No parent, looking forward to receiving and nourishing a new life, can be prepared for that rapid, harsh change of direction—the burial of their baby. While preparing to give life, no one prepares to say goodbye.

The author, in a piece written just days after her loss, expresses the bonding that takes place between a mother and her unborn baby, the change in her life that occurs early in her pregnancy, and the subsequent devastation that takes place when the baby dies.

On February 9th my precious little son was born. His birth, however, was not accompanied by the felicitations of such an occasion. This baby was born after only three months of living in my body.

I cannot possibly express all that I have felt in the past few days. Horror, bewilderment, frustration, anger, emptiness—the list goes on. But I keep trying to remember the incredible happiness that my little boy brought to me in his short life, and somehow, I feel a sort of peace.

My little boy was tiny, but he brought so much joy to so many people. Few people could ever have such a life that renders only everything that is beautiful. But for me, he was more than what could be; a mere potentiality—he was my son from the moment I knew that I was pregnant.

My life changed radically with the knowledge of my pregnancy. Typically a poor eater, I was aware of every crumb that I ate, trying to fight the nausea with the conviction that if I ate, the baby would be happy. And at night, I gagged down those necessary vitamins despite the fact that my doctor informed me that I could start taking them later. That baby was going to get those vitamins regardless of how I felt. And along those lines, I placed little white baby boots on the back of the toilet so that I would remember why I was being sick in those especially difficult moments.

I used to take walks, being content to know that my little secret companion was with me. And as I walked, I would think of how good it was for us to get some fresh air. During those walks I would talk to God and tell him of the joy I felt and how happy I was to be his partner in this miracle.

Other typically meaningless events became significant with the knowledge of my pregnancy. When I was in the car, I would change the radio station if a hard rock song came on—after all, babies shouldn't hear those kinds of things. And finally, in the evening when I would rest, I would put my hand on my barely swollen stomach, just so that we could reassure each other that the other was there.

I'll never forget seeing my son on ultrasound for the first time. The knowledge that he really was there and that he moved! By the way he used his legs, we were sure that he would be a basketball player. The day my baby died, we saw him doing flips and (what we interpreted as) waving to us. Those were the first and last pictures by which I would have to remember my baby. Those pictures, and the ones in my mind of the perfectly formed little boy in the palm of my hand. Amazing that, amidst the horror, I gazed at his beauty. After all, I knew him—he was a part of me.

Although the loss of my baby has been the most heartbreaking experience of my life, I have learned to cling to the miracle of his life on this earth. My experience with pregnancy and my brief role in motherhood has brought me closer to heaven than I ever knew was possible. And indeed, that's where I want to be. For, the way I see it, heaven just needed another angel.

Today, parents bond with their babies very early in the pregnancy. The result is a parent-infant bond that can be strong and intense, even in its earliest stages. Losing that baby can leave parents "in the lurch," being unsure of what to think or how to start the grieving and healing process. However, parents can rest assured that their feelings are normal and that help is available in their time of need.

Notes

1. Melinda Beck with Ingrid Wickelgren, Vicki Quade and Pat Wingert, "Miscarriages," *Newsweek*, August 15, 1988, p.46.

2. Denise Schipani, "Unraveling the Mystery of Miscarriage," *Child*, 1989, pp. 112, 114.

3. Beck, "Miscarriages," p. 51.

4. Ibid., p. 49.

5. Carolyn Campbell, "When Something Inside You Dies, Coping With Miscarriage," *Network*, February 1990, p. 12-13.

6. John Steinbeck, *The Grapes of Wrath* (New York: Penguin Books, 1939, 1967), p. 103.

THREE

The Grieving Process

Weeping may endure for a night, but joy cometh in the morning.
—Psalms 30:5

As Latter-day Saints, we believe that we should take hardship and tragedy in stride. Our pioneer heritage reminds us of those who face tremendous pain and suffering and still are able to sing out, "All is well." We sit in fast and testimony meetings and hear inspirational testimonies from others and think, "What's wrong with me?" or "Why is this so hard for me?" or "Where is my faith?" But what we fail to recognize is that most of these inspirational stories come from people *after* the trial of their faith. They are reporting on the spiritual blessings that can come from tragedy after the dust has settled. More than likely, the pioneers or other courageous examples all felt the same loss and despair that we feel. But the key is that they learned to overcome their trials—even grow from them—and therein lies their greatness. That is the goal when being immersed in a particular trial: to not only survive the tragedy, but to grow from the experience.

In order to grow from loss, grief is *necessary*. It is not a sign of weakness or lack of faith, but it is the first step in the arduous task of putting lives back together. Parents who are recovering from the loss of a baby should be encouraged to grieve.

They should become acquainted with the stages of the grieving process and their accompanying reactions and emotions. However, it must be realized that the grieving process can be extraordinarily difficult, invoking some of the most heart-wrenching emotions ever to be encountered by many individuals. Rene Strikwerda, whose daughter was stillborn, expresses her feelings regarding the harsh transition from being an expectant parent to a grieving parent:

The Bookstore
"Stillborn," "When Pregnancy Fails"
these words that shout at me
declaring themselves.
These hated words draw my eyes
to the bookshelf. I do not want to follow.
The titles inviting me to join
their band of broken hearts and shattered lives.
I want to scream—I do not belong here!

So few weeks ago I stood in this place
with rounded belly and lofty dreams
A joyous member of the living
hungrily absorbing information
on pregnancy and caring for baby.
The knowing smiles from women
the casual glance from belly to face
Eyes embraced you, welcoming you
to the secret club.

I choose the book on grief
and lay it on the counter like an unclean thing.
The eyes have changed. They look away
No longer wanting to see inside you.
They secret my purchase away
but I am not concealed
I have been torn open for all to see.

As I leave the bell on the door mocks me
singing "Your baby is dead."

In discussing grief and its many facets, it is important for grieving parents to know that grieving is healthy and natural, even though their own emotions and reactions may seem shocking. "I never thought I could feel or act like this" is a common statement made by grieving parents. The stages of grief serve only as a guideline; some parents may pass through all of the stages or just some of them, while for others the stages overlap. All of these experiences are normal. It is important to note, however, that while grief can surface in many different ways, suicidal or destructive feelings should not be taken lightly. If you or a loved one should have suicidal thoughts or feel as if you may harm others, please seek professional help.

Shock and Numbness
The first stage of grief is shock and numbness.[1] This period can last from forty-eight hours to two weeks. During this stage it is common to feel overwhelmed by the situation. One woman described it as if "someone had dumped a huge package upon my lap and it was my job to sort through that package and deal with what I found inside of it." This stage may include feelings of guilt, fear, anxiety, and depression. Because of these feelings the person grieving may want to sleep all of the time, or may be exhausted but unable to sleep. Other common reactions may include loss of appetite, difficulty in taking in information, and having uncontrollable emotions. It is important in this stage to express true feelings and get the grieving process underway.

Guilt is probably one of the most common reactions women have during this stage, especially if there are no medical explanations for the loss. When a baby dies, the mother tends to think in the destructive patterns of "I should have" and "What if?" Many women attribute the loss to "not getting enough rest," or "working too hard." Others feel that if they could have seen the doctor sooner or if they had noticed the symptoms or lack of movement in the baby sooner, they could have saved their child. These reactions are common in a society that tells us we can control our lives, but they can devastate a woman who is already trying to cope with the loss of her baby and does not need the destructive emotion of guilt to contend with as well. Women need to allow themselves to believe that some things are simply beyond their control and to take comfort in knowing that if given a chance, they would have done all within their power to save their baby.

Searching and Yearning

The next stage of grief is searching and yearning, which generally runs its course in a few months. During this stage, the grieving parent looks for reasons why this tragedy had to happen (beyond a medical explanation). This part of grief also involves searching for what has been lost and the feeling that maybe the baby never even existed. Many women struggle to find evidence that the baby did, indeed, pass through their life. At this point, having seen or held the baby and having pictures of it can be helpful.

Women who experience the loss of a baby often have such bizarre thoughts and emotions that they actually begin to question their own sanity. Sue, the mother of a stillborn daughter, readily admits, "There were many times in the months following the loss of our daughter when I was sure I was 'going crazy.'" Many women who are searching and yearning have dreams that someone will leave a baby on their porch, while others have strong desires to adopt a baby. Others have a desire to mother something like a puppy or a kitten. Many women actually have aching arms from their desire to hold their lost babies; others experience a "broken heart," in which their chest actually aches from the emotional trauma. Margaret, who has lost five children, recalls that it was "an indescribable pain...my chest literally hurt as if my heart really did break." Some women find it helpful to hold a doll, stuffed animal, or blanket to soothe their aching arms and heartbreak.

Other women at this stage experience phantom kicks, hear the cries of a baby, or even develop phobias. One woman who lost a baby shortly after birth explains, "I wake up in the middle of the night and think I'm pregnant. I think, 'I must be pregnant because there's no baby.'" And many women experience nightmares and other disturbing dreams for a time. But most can rest assured that they are completely normal and are dealing with the trauma of their loss successfully. In time, these bizarre experiences will subside.

Miscarriage can pose special difficulties in this stage because most women do not get to hold or even see their babies, and they do not generally have any kind of memorial for the child. Nicole, who lost her baby at twelve weeks, recalls, "I had the fatigue, the nausea, and even a little bit of a tummy with my pregnancy. My life had already significantly changed, but when that baby was gone, it was gone and I had nothing to show for the three months that child was a part of my life." Another woman explains, "When I lost my baby at the beginning of the second trimester, I had labor pains, my water broke, and the baby even came out connected to me with the umbilical cord still intact. I gave birth to that baby. And three days later, my milk came in. Yet, there was no memorial service, no outpouring of sympathy, no evidence that I gave birth to and lost a baby."

To help them cope with this difficult circumstance, women are encouraged to create a memorial for their lost babies. In a cemetery in Springfield, Illinois, a number of women, seeing the need to remember these tiny lives, made their own memorial. There is a large plot in the cemetery designated for the burial of miscarried babies. An inscription on the headstone reads: "Holy Innocents." This memorial is a gesture to validate the existence of these little ones who pass through this life all too briefly: a memorial of a very tender portion of a woman's life, never to be forgotten.

Anger is the other major component in this stage of grief. It may be directed toward anybody: yourself, your mate, your doctor, God. As one woman who had a stillborn daughter reflected, "Right after the baby's birth I was very philosophical and spiritually moved, and I spent a lot of time writing poetry. However, now I find myself becoming more and more angry and hateful and spiteful. Here I thought I was doing so well, and now I feel like this. All I know is I have been planning to stay home and be a mom this year. I have a beautiful nursery upstairs and there is supposed to be someone in it. Now what am I supposed to do?" Another woman says, "I am so angry that every day I literally scream out 'Why?'" Many people feel guilty for having such angry feelings, but anger is a very normal reaction to loss and will eventually subside. In fact, venting one's anger is actually necessary, because unexpressed anger can turn into serious depression.

One of the most common initiators of anger is the pain that many women feel when they are around other pregnant women. Because pregnancy is such an all-consuming condition, it is often difficult for other women to be considerate of the losses of other women and courteous in dealing with them. Furthermore, reminders of babies seem to crop up everywhere. One woman explained her difficulty in dealing with other pregnant women after the loss of her baby: "It seems like after you lose a baby, everyone is pregnant or is holding a newborn in their arms. Just standing in line at the grocery store can be a painful experience." Another woman expressed hostile feelings toward other pregnant women. "I was following a television show in which one of the main characters was pregnant," she said. "After I lost the baby, I honestly couldn't bear to watch that show and listen to that woman talk about her pregnancy. In fact, sometimes when I would see a pregnant woman on the street, I would want to hit her or something—I would truly hate her. How come she could have a happy, normal pregnancy and all I got was all this pain?" Still another woman expressed her frustration with pregnant women and new mothers: "I have a hard time when pregnant women complain about being uncomfortable or when a new mother complains that her baby wakes her up in the night. I would give anything to be pregnant and uncomfortable or to be awakened by a sweet little baby in the other room. These women just don't realize what they have." Finally, Joanne explains her feelings toward a friend who became pregnant shortly after her loss: "My friend couldn't understand why it was hard for me to talk about her pregnancy and be happy for her. I just couldn't—there was nothing inside me that felt happy, and what little there was I had to hold onto for myself. I know it's irrational, but I felt as if Heavenly Father took my baby away and gave it to my friend."

Disorientation and Disorganization

The third stage of grief, disorientation and disorganization, is typified by depression and lack of motivation. During this stage, which is most common in the fourth and sixth months after the loss, the grieving person may again experience overeating or lack of appetite, and may lose interest in her appearance. There may be difficulty in making decisions, withdrawal, and a reluctance to go out.

One woman who had lost a baby found comfort in sitting in the shower for hours because it was a small, cozy area. Another woman found herself sitting at work and staring into space for long periods of time without realizing that any time had elapsed. Still another woman became frustrated because the people around her were insisting that she "get out of the house." She found this to be an invasion of her privacy and "just wanted to be left alone." This lack of motivation can make any woman feel as if her life is on hold. As Nancy explains, "I feel like I'm in a stalled car and the rest of the traffic keeps going by. It doesn't seem right that the world just keeps going." Another woman adds, "After I lost my baby, I felt as if I was in a bumper car like those at amusement parks—I would just go to wherever I was bumped."

Another common reaction during this period is feeling like a failure as a woman. This is particularly true in our Latter-day Saint culture where the role of mother is so important. The female is seen as the "giver of life," and as one woman put it, "Everyone is supposed to be able to do it." To many women, having children is the essence of womanhood; and when a woman loses a baby, it is common for her to feel as if she has failed her husband, her family, herself, her baby, and has, in general, failed as a woman. As one woman states, "Here is something that all my friends and neighbors could do and I couldn't. One woman even said to me 'You should know how to do this by now'. But having children isn't something you know." Another woman explains, "I felt that I had let my baby down, and I felt like I should apologize to him for not being a good enough mother to even get him to this earth."

The feeling of failure can lead to a total loss of self-esteem. Suddenly, the woman becomes unsure of her abilities in all aspects of her life. After going through a miscarriage, one woman explained that she lost confidence in herself to be successful at anything. "I was typically willing to try new things and I was confident that I could accomplish new things," she said. "After losing my baby, I was afraid to do even the simplest task because I was sure I would fail."

Hand in hand with the lack of self-esteem that often accompanies the death of a baby is the feeling of a loss of control. For women who are in strict control of their lives at all times, losing a baby is a painful reminder of how little control over their lives they do have. As one woman explains, "For the first time, I wanted something and yet I had no control over getting it." Another woman states, "It was difficult to know that things were happening to my body and my baby, and there was nothing I could do about it."

An emotional domino effect continues as lack of self-esteem gives rise to a feeling of vulnerability. This occurs not only during a pregnancy following the loss, but in all other aspects of a woman's life. "Usually the bad things seem to happen to other people, but here I had been a victim of a horrible experience, and I felt like anything could happen to me. I learned that there are no guarantees in life," explains Linda. "When my husband would come home late for dinner, instead of assuming that he had gotten held up at the office, or that he was stuck in traffic like I used to, I immediately panicked and thought that something terrible had happened to him for sure. By the time he did come home I was hysterical." Nancy adds, "I used to read the news of cancer and other illnesses and not think twice about them. Now I feel as if anything can happen, and I'm scared."

Reorganization

The final stage of grief is reorganization, which can take months to achieve. At this point, the grieving person realizes that life does indeed go on and is finally able to enjoy life again with a renewed energy and without feeling guilty. Most people who have recently experienced a loss cannot even imagine feeling whole again. Yet it does happen; peace and joy once again become a part of life. In this stage, life is no longer a series of mechanical actions and there is often a sense of release.

Reorganization means that the parents come to accept the death of the baby and resolve those feelings to a point where it is once more possible to participate actively in life. Of course, this reorganization does not mean that the pain goes away completely. The parents will be changed forever by their loss and will always have a tender place in their hearts. Daily life becomes enjoyable again, but it should come as no surprise when certain events trigger sadness. Remember that anniversaries of the baby's death, due dates, holidays, a school play or other children's performances can still be difficult. Just a song on the radio or a certain sight or smell can bring back feelings of sadness. Many parents find comfort in celebrating the baby's birthday, having a special trip to the cemetery, going to the temple, or purchasing a special memento to cope with those days.

The positive aspect of this stage is that many parents are able to look back on the experience and concentrate on the happiness of the pregnancy, or even find good things that have come out of the loss. As one woman explains, "I used to feel that if I caught myself laughing at something, going to a social function, or even making love, I was betraying the memory of my baby. After all, how could I enjoy myself if I truly cared about him? But then I realized he would want me to be happy, and the memories of him should be pleasant too."

Some couples find specific blessings that have come out of their tragedy. One woman states, "Tragedy can bond a marriage in a way nothing else can. My husband and I are closer now than we have ever been." Other people find a renewed belief in God. Says Molly, who had a miscarriage, "I don't know why God took my baby, but I do know that he helped me cope with the loss. I have come to a new realization of God's love and mercy." Maureen states, "I am sure that I am a better mother because of the loss of our first baby. I see each of my children as a miracle and I love them all the more." And

Lisa, who has had nine miscarriages, states that "there is no way you can go through the loss of a baby without coming out of that loss a better person. You become more loving, more caring, more compassionate, and generally kinder because you have learned the hard way what a miracle life is."

Perhaps the most exciting element in this stage is that the true greatness and resilience of the human spirit becomes apparent in many lives. Those who endure tragedy can claim to have truly lived—to have experienced every possible human emotion in the spectrum. Those who survive tragedy join the elite group of mankind who have suffered and triumphed over the depths of despair.

Emerging as survivors, parents are privy, if they desire, to a special understanding of God's plan. The scriptures and the teachings of Christ take on new significance, and Christ's suffering in Gethsemane and on the cross assumes new meaning. For an individual who has tasted such pain, the intense suffering of Christ comes into clearer perspective and becomes infinitely more personal. Furthermore, an appreciation of the gift his suffering rendered—eternal life—takes on new depth and beauty.

To experience the full spectrum of the most heart-wrenching emotions in the human experience and to still emerge triumphant is, indeed, a miracle. Clearly, Christ is working in the lives of all those who pass through tribulation. Although there may be little control over the events that take place in life, Christ provides the power to overcome them. No one is alone. As Walt Whitman said, "Every moment of light and dark is a miracle."

Notes

1. Information on the stages of grief from SHARE, "When a Baby Dies" (pamphlet).

FOUR

Tools for Grieving Parents

Come unto me, all ye that labour and are heavy laden, and I will give you rest. Take my yoke upon you, and learn of me; for I am meek and lowly in heart: and ye shall find rest unto your souls. For my yoke is easy, and my burden is light.
—Matthew 11:28-30

If you are a parent who has lost a baby, you may be wondering if there are specific things you can do to help ease the pain associated with the grieving process. While there is nothing that can shorten the process, there are some things you can do to facilitate your emotional recovery.

Pamper yourself. Allow yourself any luxury you can—you deserve it. Buy yourself a new outfit, go out to dinner or a movie, spend time alone; do whatever makes you happy. Remember that taking care of yourself does not mean you have forgotten your baby; it is a way of coping. And be sure to have a regular physical exam. Some physicians believe that parents who have experienced an emotional trauma have an above-average risk for illness.

Find a strong and loving support system. Family members and friends can be a great source of comfort during a difficult time. However, it also helps to talk to people who have been through the same kind of tragedy and have experienced emotions and challenges similar to yours. Through your hospital or health care professional, seek support groups and, if you desire, appropriate counseling.

Trust yourself and your judgment. When a baby dies, there are several decisions that need to be made. Some women feel like they are being strange if they want to see and hold their baby after its death. However, health care professionals are now realizing the importance of this time between the parents and their child. Experts say that parents' thoughts and fears about how the baby will look are often much worse than the reality. Parents are also encouraged to take pictures and to keep the baby with them for awhile in their room. In some cases, there are burial and memorial service issues to be handled. Do those things you think are appropriate, and do not worry about being strange. Your grief is yours alone, and only you know how to handle it. One woman who lost a baby at birth recalls, "My husband and I went up to the hospital to dress the baby for the burial, even though everyone told us not to. I'll admit sometimes it's hard for me to think about it, but I'm really glad that we did that."

Accept each stage of grief. Rather than fighting the emotions that accompany grief, go through those stages willingly and realize that by doing so, you will resolve your grief more easily. Many people feel guilty about being angry or depressed; but remember, those emotions are completely normal. At the funeral of a friend, one woman who had previously lost a baby was shocked when a speaker said there was no reason to grieve because of their religious beliefs. "I believe in the gospel and it's a great comfort to me," she said, "but I still hurt so bad I didn't know what to do. It didn't matter where my baby was in the afterlife. The fact was, she wasn't with me." Many people interpret sorrow and despair to be a lack of faith in Heavenly Father and in the gospel. Remember that regardless of how devoted you are to the gospel, death hurts; and the grieving process is necessary to be able to find joy in life again.

Give your baby a name. Many people find comfort in naming their baby regardless of its gestational age. By doing so, you are showing that your baby was a real person and entitled to acknowledgment.

Write a letter to your baby. It can be very therapeutic to write all your feelings down in a letter to your baby. What would you like him to know? What would you tell him if he were here?

Envision yourself giving your baby to Christ. This may sound unusual, but many women have found peace in actually envisioning themselves placing their babies in the Savior's arms. This mental exercise seems to take some of the fear out of death, and gives comforting assurance to the parent that the baby is in good hands until they are together again.

Cherish the memories of your pregnancy and your baby. Try to remember the happy times in your pregnancy and the positive and loving feelings you have for your child. As was previously mentioned, some women struggle with the issue of "Did my baby exist?" Even when a baby is lost through stillbirth or infant death and a memorial service is performed, the brief life of the child can seem like a blur to many parents. It then becomes important to them to have proof that their baby did indeed exist, and to concentrate on happier memories. As one mother explains, "We all find it so important to 'gather evidence' to prove our child's existence and the impact it had on our lives. Whether that means completing a baby book for the lost child, writing poetry to the baby or collecting mementos from the hospital, it is important for others to know that this was a *child* that was lost."

One woman who had a stillborn daughter kept a special box containing mementos of her daughter's birth. Contained in the box were the hat put on the baby following her birth, a corner of the blanket she had in the hospital and was subsequently buried in, and pictures the hospital took of the infant. Explains one mother of a stillborn son, "I thought it was morbid and disgusting when a friend of mine had a stillborn child and had the picture of the baby displayed. But that is exactly what I am going to do with the pictures of my son. He is as important to me as my other children, and not a mere memory that I would like to forget."

Following her miscarriage, one woman put together a special book containing writing she had done including a letter to the baby, ultrasound pictures of the baby, and other special pictures and thoughts she had collected that were a comfort to her. "This was the most significant experience of my life," she observes, "and I want to remember it in a positive way and have some memorial to my baby." Other women find comfort in planting a tree or a flower to memorialize their baby, or by having the birthstone of their baby set into a piece of jewelry they can wear. Finally, one woman explains the necessity of selecting a headstone for her stillborn daughter's grave: "It's the last thing I can do for my daughter—I've got to have that headstone."

Put an obituary in the paper. This is a statement to the world that your baby lived and died, and that its life was—and is—important to you.

Keep a journal. Many people find it helpful to record their feelings in a journal. Oftentimes people feel uncomfortable telling others all of their thoughts and feelings, and writing them down is a great way of expressing them. It is important that entries be honest and not try to be "noble." This is the only way that difficult emotions and issues can be worked through. A journal can also be helpful after the crisis is over. It can be surprising and gratifying to see your progress since each entry was made.

Seek spiritual guidance. If you have doctrinal or spiritual questions, or are in need of comfort, seek helpful books or writings from the prophets or other church leaders. If you need help more specific to your individual situation, seek counsel from your bishop.

Welcome priesthood blessings. Priesthood blessings can provide peace, comfort, and direction. Blessings can also give the father of the baby a tangible way to help.

Whenever possible, put off making any major decisions. Decisions such as a job or residence change are best made when you have had sufficient time to resolve your grief. Hasty decisions made in moments of deep grief may be problematic later.

Try to be patient with others. Remember that people deal with grief differently, and many people will not react in the way you expect them to. Others may make insensitive comments that may even seem cruel. It is unfortunate that in a crisis bereaved parents must deal with the insensitivity of others, but most people do not mean to be hurtful. One way of alleviating awkward feelings towards others is to be honest with them about how you feel and tell them gently when they hurt you. By being open, you not only take a step in resolving your relations with others, but you can do your part in educating society about the tragedy of the loss of a baby.

Help other women. After experiencing something so traumatic as the loss of your baby, you are uniquely prepared to take your wisdom and help others in a similar situation. One woman who lost a baby years ago, visits her daughter's grave only on occasion, but she has not forgotten her. She takes every opportunity to speak out about her tragedy, inform others, and help other women who have lost a baby. By doing so, she believes that she symbolically "puts flowers on her baby's grave."

Believe in Christ

Perhaps the greatest tool we have to help us conquer our trials is the Savior himself. When in the midst of despair, we can lean on the scripture in Proverbs: "Trust in the Lord with all thine heart; and lean not unto thine own understanding. In all thy ways acknowledge him, and he shall direct thy paths" (Proverbs 3:5-6).

As darkness seems to become all-encompassing, perhaps the only recourse available is simply to trust in the Lord. Trust that he is, that he is guiding our lives on the path he sees fit—perhaps a path that in a previous time we agreed to follow. Or perhaps it is a path chosen by these babies so that they may fulfill their own special missions. Someday we will know the truth and the whole picture of the Lord's eternal plan for us. Until then, bitterness cannot be allowed to mar the beauty of the lives of these pure, innocent babies. If we can continue to communicate with the Lord through prayer, seek his wisdom through the scriptures, and heed the words of the prophet and other present-day leaders, we will find peace. He will not forsake us if we earnestly turn to him and allow ourselves to be encircled by his loving arms.

The words of a beautiful hymn tell of turning to the Lord when darkness fills our lives, and the subsequent peace we can find through him:

> Abide with me; 'tis eventide.
> The day is past and gone;
> The shadows of the evening fall;
> The night is coming on.
> Within my heart a welcome guest,
> Within my home abide.
> O Savior, stay this night with me;
> Behold, 'tis eventide.
> O Savior, stay this night with me;
> Behold, 'tis eventide.
>
> Abide with me; 'tis eventide.
> Thy walk today with me

Has made my heart within me burn,
As I communed with thee.
Thy earnest words have filled my soul
And kept me near thy side.
O Savior, stay this night with me;
Behold, 'tis eventide.
O Savior, stay this night with me;
Behold, 'tis eventide.

Abide with me; 'tis eventide,
And lone will be the night
If I cannot commune with thee,
Nor find thee in my light.
The darkness of the world, I fear,
Would in my home abide.
O Savior, stay this night with me;
Behold 'tis eventide.
O Savior, stay this night with me;
Behold, 'tis eventide.

Text: Lowrie M. Hofford, Music: Harrison Millard
(LDS Hymns, No. 165)

There is no reason for us to feel at any time that we must face our challenges alone. He is with us, he knows us, and through him we will find peace.

When to Try Again

Children born after a loss have been referred to as "rainbow babies" because they are considered to be the beautiful rainbow that follows the storm. But knowing when to have that baby can be difficult. One woman expressed her feelings about waiting to have another baby after her loss:

The suitcase is waiting, for some time next year.
The suitcase is waiting, with Carter's undershirts

size 3 months and birth announcements
and nightgowns that button down the front.
Yesterday I noticed that one latch had come undone
and it had partially opened up and
the nightgowns were spilling out.
The suitcase is waiting, but not very patiently.

Marion Cohen, from "She Was Born She Died" (Centering Corp.) and "An Ambitious Sort of Grief" (the Liberal Press).

After the draining experience of losing a baby and going through the difficult grieving process, many couples wonder if there is a right time to have another baby. Many women and men look with dread at the months of waiting during a pregnancy. And yet, despite the deep fear, many couples are anxious to try again. Still, some couples feel that getting pregnant again too soon would "dishonor" the memory of the baby they lost. This unusual mixture of emotions can lead to great confusion. On one hand, you want so badly to be pregnant again; and on the other, it is your worst nightmare.

Deciding when to have another baby is an extremely personal decision. Some people need more time to even consider the possibility of another pregnancy; for others, it is the thought of another baby that keeps them going. Although there are no set rules, here are a few guidelines that may help you to know when the time is right.[1]

Take time to recover physically from your previous pregnancy. Your body went through many changes with your pregnancy and delivery, and it requires time to recover from the experience. Readiness depends on the type of pregnancy and delivery you had before, conditions that caused complications in your previous pregnancy that need to be remedied, your age, number of previous pregnancies, and your general health. Discuss the option of another pregnancy with your physician.

Take time for emotional recovery. Grieving is a long, difficult process that takes a lot of energy. Pregnancy takes a lot of energy as well. Be certain you can handle both tasks simultaneously. Also, make sure the baby you are going to have is not just a replacement for the one you lost. Have your baby for the right reasons.

Find out as much as you can about the causes of your baby's death. By researching the causes of your baby's death, you will be well-informed about the possible risks of your subsequent pregnancy. In your research, you may be able to discover treatments and procedures that could prevent the same tragedy from occurring again. In many cases, the cause of death is unknown; but in some instances, certain steps can be taken that may help. Finding out as much as you can about your loss may help you to put some fears to rest, and may help you to regain some confidence and control.

When you do become pregnant again, it is normal to be frightened and very anxious. But by following good prenatal health guidelines and the advice of your physician, you can take comfort in knowing that you are doing all within your power to ensure your baby's health.

There will probably be many issues to be worked out with your subsequent pregnancy. Remember that having another baby does not mean that you love your lost baby any less. Try to write down and discuss your feelings; and above all, take time to relax and enjoy yourself.

Some people may say to you, "You're not going to get pregnant again soon, are you?" But remember that family planning is a very personal issue, and only you know when the time is right. One woman who lost a baby and became pregnant right away said, "Getting pregnant finally got me thinking about life again instead of death. Instead of counting the months' anniversary of the death of my first baby, I was counting how many months pregnant I was."

Notes

1. "Thinking About Another Pregnancy" (pamphlet), The Childbirth and Parent Education Association for Bereaved Parents Support Group, 1016 Van Buren, Madison, Wisconsin 53711, 1978.

FIVE

A Father's Grief

And he shall turn the heart of the fathers to the children. —3 Nephi 25:6

It is widely believed that experiencing a tragedy within a marriage will do one of two things: bond the marriage closer than ever or pull those bonds slowly apart. Either there is a tenderness and an understanding within the marriage as the couple shares in this grief, or there is tension and anger which could result in yet another tragedy: the loss of the marriage. In any kind of tragedy or stress within a marriage, divorce is not an uncommon result.

It is interesting to note, when talking to couples who have recently experienced a loss, what their body language can indicate. One can often discern how the tragedy is affecting their marriage simply by observing how they sit. If they are leaning on each other physically, they are usually leaning on each other emotionally. Many hold hands and touch each other. Conversely, many sit a couple of feet apart from each other. Again, if they are turning against each other physically, they are usually turning against each other emotionally. Some parents even attend support groups alone—perhaps a sign that there is not a united front in battling their grief.

Many of the problems that can occur in a marriage

following a tragedy can be attributed to society's lack of interest regarding a father's grief, as well as differences in the way a man and a woman grieve. These differences can give way to misunderstanding and insensitivity toward the father as he fulfills his role in the best way he knows how.

The Overlooked Partner

Today, the father of the child is encouraged to be involved in the pregnancy and birth experience. Not only is he encouraged to be present at the birth of the child, where he is allowed to cut the umbilical cord, hold, and sometimes bathe the baby, but his presence and support are also becoming valued contributions during the months leading up to the birth. Men are encouraged to accompany their wives to prenatal appointments, read literature on pregnancy, and attend prenatal classes. Perhaps one of the most bonding experiences a man can have is to see his child on ultrasound. While a woman can feel the baby inside her, it is usually quite a revelation for the father to see that his child really does exist and move. It can even be shocking for a father to see that his baby actually looks like a baby!

While these advances in attitudes are helpful and encourage the father-child relationship, what happens to that relationship when something goes wrong in the pregnancy and the baby dies? In this event, the father of the child is often overlooked. Although society may not completely understand the bond between a mother and a child, society does not even acknowledge the father-child relationship at all. As one woman states, "It really hurt me after we lost our baby to have people walk past my husband to give me a hug. No one even thought that he might be hurting too."

Many issues must be considered when examining the grief of a father. One sensitive mother-in-law, seeing the difficult issues regarding men and grief, wrote this poem to her son-in-law after his baby girl was stillborn:

To Brett

It must be very difficult
To be a man in grief,
Since "men don't cry" and "men are strong"
No tears can bring relief.

It must be very difficult
To stand up to the test
And field calls and visitors
So she can get some rest.

They always ask if she's all right
And what she's going through,
But seldom take his hand and ask,
"My friend, but how are you?"
He hears her crying in the night
And thinks his heart will break.
He dries her tears and comforts her,
But "stays strong" for her sake.

It must very difficult
To start each day anew
And try to be so very brave—
He lost his baby too.

Eileen Knight Hagemeister

Silence is Golden?

Little boys are raised to believe that "real men don't cry," and that they should "buck up." Women, on the other hand, are encouraged to cry and to talk. These differences in the socialization of men and women can lead to conflict in many areas of marriage, and they cause particular misunderstanding in the face of tragedy. While the man is being stoic and "strong," the woman may perceive this to mean that he is not grieving. This naturally leads to anger and frustration within the marriage. One woman observes, "I would keep nagging my husband to talk to me and he wouldn't. So I would assume that he wasn't feeling anything, and I felt very alone."

When a man finally does realize that he is not as strong as he thinks he should be and that he must confront his grief, he can face serious self-esteem problems. A man's show of emotion can cause him to think, "What's wrong with me? I'm not supposed to feel this way," rather than accepting it as a normal reaction. Many men even begin to feel that they are failing as husbands because they are demonstrating what they perceive to be weakness.

The Role of Protector

Most men feel that they are responsible to protect their wives and children. Typically when a couple loses a baby, the father is concerned not only for the loss of his child but for the well-being of his wife. Because he is concerned for his wife, who has undergone physical as well as emotional trauma, the father of the child may work hard to keep things "business as usual" to give his wife some kind of normalcy in her world. As in the poem "To Brett," the father often tries to shield the mother from continued pain, himself facing the never-ending and often unfeeling questions from outsiders. It is often the father who takes care of practical matters after a loss, such as funeral arrangements, medical matters, and financial decisions.

Unlike the mother of the child, who is given a brief "grace period" to grieve, the father is expected to be able to deal with the public and carry on with his life as if nothing had happened. Furthermore, a man may feel an obligation to keep his feelings about the loss of the child from his wife in order to shield her from witnessing his pain. These expectations can cause a man to feel that his emotions of grief are abnormal and make him uncomfortable about expressing them. In fact, a man can face a no-win situation: While some women have difficulty with their husbands' reluctance to share their feelings, other women seem to find it even more difficult to deal with their show of emotion. One woman expresses it this way: "I kept asking my husband what he felt and was angry that he wouldn't share his feelings with me. But I have to admit, when I finally did see him cry, it almost tore me apart."

Still other complications can develop from this assumed role of protector. Some men also feel like a failure when they are unable to comfort their wife and feel helpless when they can't "make the hurt go away." One man states, "It was really difficult when my wife would be upset and she would turn away from me. For the first time in our marriage I couldn't help her. I felt like I was really failing her." Another man whose wife has had several miscarriages explains, "Every time my wife loses a baby, I lose another part of her. There's nothing I can do to help."

On the Job

Going back to work is one of the most difficult events a man must face after the loss of his baby. Many men find it difficult to concentrate and resent having to be at work. They may stare into space when work should be done and make more mistakes than usual. Some men find it especially difficult because of the lack of empathy they face from their coworkers. If anything is said about the tragedy, it is usually a question about the well-being of the wife. States one father who had a stillborn baby, "While my wife's office sent flowers, mine didn't do anything. I went back to work, and no one said a word to me. It was as if nothing had even happened." Another father struggled with the fact that after his wife experienced the miscarriage of their first baby, she received special consideration on Mother's Day, but he was not even acknowledged on Father's Day. "No one said anything to me or even gave me a card; no one even felt that I was a father, except for me."

Conversely, some men deal with their grief by becoming absorbed with their work. While working, the man is forced to think about something else; therefore, many men find comfort in spending long hours at the office. While work may serve as a comfortable diversion, total absorption in work may prevent some men from dealing adequately with their grief or the grief of others involved. Some men work long hours to avoid confronting the uncomfortable situation at home. Says one father of a stillborn son, "It's on the way home from work that the whole crisis hits me; then I have to go home and see my wife hurt."

How Do Men Grieve?

So the question remains: How and when do men grieve? Men tend to express their grief openly when their wives are not around. Most of the time a man's grief is demonstrated in more subtle ways; a man can be grieving and no one would suspect it. While women tend to cry, men tend to demonstrate anger. Many men experience irritability and short tempers. One man explains, "I often find myself getting upset at things that never used to bother me before. I find myself yelling at other motorists." Because men like to physically deal with problems they may, as one man put it, have a desire to "beat someone up." Therefore, some men engage in the martial arts, jogging, or other physical exercise.

Some men may feel the need to internalize their feelings, which can lead to serious health problems. One man developed an ulcer after his wife miscarried their son because he resisted demonstrating his sorrow. Other men develop headaches and chest pains due to anxiety. Rather than compound their problems with illness, men need to learn how to deal with their grief properly.

To facilitate the confrontation of grief and the grieving process, men can follow some simple guidelines:

Talk about your feelings. It sounds trite, but talking about your grief really can help. If you do not feel comfortable talking to your wife, discuss your feelings with a friend, counselor, bishop, or other man who has lost a child. If you are reluctant to talk to your wife, it is often helpful to at least tell her why you feel that way, thereby alleviating some of the tension in your marriage. Most women would agree that although it is difficult knowing your husband hurts too, it at least helps to know that he is feeling something.

Channel your anger properly. Since men often grieve by showing anger, be careful that you do not take your anger out on your wife and surviving children. Channel your anger by engaging in physical activity such as athletics, yard work, etc., or again, by talking to someone who will accept your anger.

Allow yourself to cry. Crying can be the first step in resolving your feelings. Go ahead and cry in private if you must, but do not fight to keep your feelings inside—that is how health problems and misdirected anger can originate.

Do not place blame. While wanting to blame someone is a completely normal reaction to loss, no one is really to blame. Studies show that most women suffer from extreme guilt after losing a baby, and they do not need reaffirmation of those feelings from a husband. Also, doctors and hospitals are not perfect, and they can only do so much. Remember that losing a baby is a hard lesson that teaches us how very little control we have in our lives, and placing blame is only ineffective and hurtful.

Be patient with your wife. Remember that the mother-infant bond is a very intimate one, and can start at the very beginning of the pregnancy. Some men grieve just as much as their wives; others become impatient with the attention the woman gives to the loss. Be sure to give your wife the time she feels is necessary to cope with the loss of your baby.

Make your own memorial. Most men leave the scrapbooks and more tender-hearted things up to their wives, but making your own personal memorial can be a great valve for releasing pent-up feelings. Some ideas might be to write a letter, plant a tree or flower, or build something for the baby. Whatever your interest, an actual piece of work can really be helpful for men who deal better with more tangible, physical things.

Finally, there are things that a couple can do together to ease the strain:

Pray together. When kneeling together and holding hands in prayer, it becomes difficult to harbor angry feelings toward one another. Pray for understanding—and pray for each other.

If possible, attend the temple together. Nothing puts life into perspective better than reviewing why we are here and our Heavenly Father's plan for us. And we are probably never closer to those loved ones who have gone before us than when we are in the temple.

Attend support groups. Support groups can be very helpful in resolving problems associated with your loss. Meeting other couples (especially men) who are experiencing similar emotions can be very helpful. Even if you feel you have resolved your grief, attend a support group with your wife if she feels it is necessary. Doing so will give you greater insight into the emotions your wife may be having, and perhaps you will find renewed patience with the situation at home. Your grief should be a partnership, and as long as one of you has not resolved your feelings, the other partner should be supportive.

Realize that you grieve differently. Accept the differences in the way and length of time you each grieve.

Keep dating. Spending time alone together and doing things you enjoy can be a pleasant diversion from your grief.

Talk about better times. You have shared much together

before the death of your baby, and those memories can help sustain you in your loss. Talk about the time you first met, how you fell in love, and other pleasant memories.

Maintain a sense of humor. It may seem next to impossible, but maintaining a sense of humor can soften even the most difficult situation. Remember old jokes, funny memories, even silly nicknames. Others may think you are strange, but a light moment at the right time can be a blessing and a relief.

Touch and hold each other. This is a time when you need to reaffirm your love with the tender caring that a gentle touch can give.

The death of your baby is the loss of something very special, but it does not mean that you have to lose your marriage too. If you remember to give one another space and sincere caring, you could very well come out of this tragedy with an even stronger bond. After all, your loss is one that only you and your spouse share completely.

SIX

The Special Grief of Grandparents and Siblings

I will turn their mourning into joy, and will comfort them, and make them rejoice from their sorrow. —Jeremiah 31:13

When a child dies, parents are often so consumed with their own grief that they fail to see the grief of others who are also mourning. Most often, these other mourners include the grandparents of the child, as well as surviving siblings. There are special needs and unique circumstances surrounding each type of grief.

Bereaved Grandparents

If you are a grandparent to the baby, you may be facing an especially difficult situation. You not only grieve for your grandchild, but you also grieve for your child and your child's spouse, who are hurting so badly. You may be at a loss as to how to comfort them. Furthermore, the pain a grandparent experiences often goes unacknowledged. One mother put into words the unique pain she felt for her daughter at the time of the death of her granddaughter:

To Bereaved Grandparents

I am powerlessness. I am helplessness. I am frustration.
I sit with her and I cry with her. She cries for her

daughter and I cry for mine. I can't help her. I can't reach inside and take her broken heart. I must watch her suffer day after day and see her desolation.

I listen to her tell me over and over how she misses Emily, how she wants her back. I can't bring Emily back for her. I can't buy her an even better Emily than she had, like I could buy her an even better toy when she was a child.

I can't kiss the hurt and make it go away. I can't even kiss a small part of it away. There's no bandaid large enough to cover her bleeding heart.

There was a time I could listen to her talk about a fickle boyfriend and tell her it would be okay, and know in my heart that in two weeks she wouldn't even think of him. Can I tell her it'll be okay in two years when I know it will never be okay, that she will carry this pain of "what might have been" in her deepest heart for the rest of her life?

I see this young woman, my child, who was once carefree and fun-loving and bubbling with life, slumped in a chair with her eyes full of agony. Where is my power now? Where is my mother's bag of tricks that will make it all better?

Why can't I join her in the aloneness of her grief? As tight as my arms wrap around her, I can't reach that aloneness.

Where are the magic words that will give her comfort? What chapter in Dr. Spock tells me how to do this? He has told me everything else I've needed to know. Where are the answers? I should have them. I'm the mother.

What can I give her to make her better? A cold wet wash cloth will ease that swelling of her crying eyes, but it won't stop the reason for her tears. What treat will bring joy back to her? What prize will bring that "happy child" smile back again?

I know that someday she'll find happiness again. I can hold out hope for her someday, but what about now? this hour? this day?

I can give her my love and my prayers and my care and

my concern. I could give her my life. But even that won't
help.

Margaret Gerner, From *For Bereaved Grandparents*
(pamphlet) The Centering Corp.
P.O. Box 3367, Omaha, Nebraska 68103

This piece clearly illustrates the particular anguish that a
grandparent can feel. As a grandparent, your heart aches for
the precious grandchild for whom you formed your own
dreams and plans. As a mother or father, your heart aches for
the deep pain your grieving child is experiencing. Parents do
feel that they should be able to "make things better" and "fix
whatever is broken"—even if their child is an adult.

Many grandparents are taken by complete surprise at the
death of their grandbaby. Like the parents of the baby, with all
the excited plans for a new arrival, it never occurs to them that
something could go wrong. So how do you begin to heal yourself, and how do you help your grieving child?

Steps Toward Healing

In her book *For Bereaved Grandparents,* Margaret Gerner
explores the opportunities and blessings that can await many
parents who are anxious to assist their grieving children:

As a parent of a grieving child, you have the unique
opportunity to cement a deep and lasting relationship with
your child.
*   You have the opportunity to walk with your child
through the most difficult life experience they will ever
endure.
*   You have the opportunity to help your child in a very
special way and the bond that forms will never be broken.[1]

There are many things that grandparents can do to deal
with their own grief while helping the parents deal with theirs:

Be supportive by respecting the parents' decisions. Most parents and experts agree that the best role for grandparents to

take is a supportive one. Many grandparents want to shield their children from painful decisions and sometimes want to take charge of the situation. But grandparents need to remember that some of these very decisions are the ones that will start the parents on the road toward emotional recovery. Even if their decisions make you uncomfortable, remember that the parents of the baby need to grieve and demonstrate their grief in whatever way necessary.

The issue of a funeral or memorial service is a good example of the differences of opinion that can occur in the aftermath of a baby's death. Some grandparents are opposed to a service of any kind because of the baby's gestational age, or they are worried about the expense of such a service. But grandparents need to remember that this is the only thing the parents will ever be able to do for their child. If having a service is important to the parents, ask how you can help with the plans, or, if you desire, even with the expenses.

Do not interfere. Being supportive means that you do not interfere with any decisions or tasks that need to be done. Before you start putting the nursery away, ask the parents what their wishes are. In an attempt to help the parents, you can end up robbing them of a tender experience that they may need, and it can be reason for resentment years down the road.

Listen. Let your child talk as much as necessary, even if it means you hear the same stories over and over. That is how parents work through difficult issues and, ultimately, through the grief. One woman whose daughter lost a baby said, "I was really worried about how she was going to make it through this grief. However, I was happy to see that she would talk to me about what happened. When I saw that she was talking, I knew that she would be okay."

Cry with your child. Many parents of grieving children are frustrated because they do not know what to say. But crying with your child lets them know that you are aligned with them in their grief. Many parents worry needlessly that they will upset their child if they show their grief. But knowing that you share the same feelings can be a great source of comfort to your child. Cry together, and let your child know that you understand and feel a similar grief and pain.

Hold or hug your child. Many parents of a lost baby have a desire to let "Mommy" or "Daddy" take care of them and make the hurt go away like when they were a child. Your physical touch can be very comforting.

Be available. Try to spend time with your grieving child and his or her spouse, and let them know that you would be glad to stay with them. At the same time, give them the space they need to adjust to this rapid change of direction in their lives.

Ask them how you can help. Be specific in your questions. "Would you like me to make dinner? Vacuum? Tend the children?" Being specific helps them to deal with the practical matters that they find so difficult to concentrate on.

Make something as a memorial to the baby. This can be a great comfort to the grieving parents as well as to you. If you are talented in writing, needlepoint, quilting, gardening, woodworking, etc., these can be great ways to show your love. If you do not have a particular hobby that applies, you could buy clothing for the baby to be buried in, or make your own scrapbook or journal of your thoughts and feelings.

Be patient with the parents' grief. Because parents are so anxious to see their child happy, many grandparents become impatient with their child's grief. The grandparents want to put the tragedy behind them, and often feel that the parents of the baby who died are needlessly hanging on to pointless grief. Be assured that the parents are only using the time they need in order to move on with their lives. A parent's grief can even take a couple of years. Give them the time they need.

If you live far away, take special measures. If you live some distance from your grieving child, you may have to take special pains to show that you care. If possible, arrange a trip to see your child. Try to send special letters, cards, flowers, or gifts to let them know you are thinking about them.

Do not blame the parents for the baby's death. Even if the parent did not handle the pregnancy the way you thought it should be handled, do not place blame. Many grandparents are angry because they think the baby's mother got pregnant too soon, or worked too hard, or didn't eat right. Most definitely, these things had absolutely nothing to do with the death of the baby. Grieving parents do not need to hear, "I told you so."

Include the baby in family memories. Try to make mention of the baby, referring to it by name on special occasions, holidays, or family get-togethers. This can be helpful to you as well as the grieving parents, and says that this life was important to you.

Do not be angry at your own life. Some grandparents are angry that their grandbaby died while they are still alive. Such a tragedy seems to go against everything we would expect: older people die, but babies have a whole lifetime ahead of them. Try to work through your anger so that you can be of assistance to your grieving children.

Expect a change in attitudes. Don't be surprised if the announcement of a new grandchild leaves you uneasy, frightened, or simply not as excited as usual. You have been dealt a cruel blow, and you know how tenuous life can be. Eventually, you will be able to find room in your heart for both the baby who has died and those who are yet to come.

Be sure to take care of your own grief. Many grandparents become so consumed with their child's grief that they forget to address their own. This can hinder your ability to help your child. Take care of yourself and your own needs. If you would like to hold the baby, have a part in the funeral, or give the baby a special gift for the funeral, be sure to talk to your children and let them know of your desires. But try to be understanding, too, if they have a difference of opinion.

As the grandparent, your role can be a very important one in the lives of the grieving parents. You are needed, and you can be a stable and comforting influence at this difficult time. Be sure to give the parents the room they need and trust their judgment. You can bring peace to your child in a time of despair, and you can come out of this tragedy with an even deeper and more enduring relationship.

Helping Children

It is important for parents and others involved with the family to help the surviving children cope with the loss of their sibling. These children can also be forgotten or overlooked, even though they are experiencing pain as well. Even very young children are affected by the loss of a baby and deal with the loss in their own way.

How Children Show Grief

There are many differences in the way adults and children grieve. Because children may not have the understanding or verbal skills to express what they are feeling, they must work through grief in their own ways.

After one woman had miscarried one of several babies, her little four-year old son, feeling the need to talk to someone, yet feeling unable to approach his mother, went around to the neighbors explaining that "his baby" had died. When his mother questioned his actions, he replied, "Mommy, it hurts so bad." Another mother of a five-year old daughter noticed some of her daughter's artwork after their second daughter was stillborn. The girl explained that she had been drawing a picture of a "happy house." When the mother asked, "Is it our house?" the daughter replied, "No, mommy. Our house is a sad house because you cry all the time."

Finally, one little boy whose baby sister was stillborn, tenderly and insightfully expressed through poetry those concerns typical of a seven-year old regarding death:

Mary Catherine
You were like a caterpillar
Who turned into a beautiful butterfly
then went to heaven to be with God.
What's it like up there, Mary Catherine?
Do you grow when you're in heaven?
Will you have birthdays?
I'll never forget you and I love you
As if you were alive and with us.

Todd Jordan

In all of these cases, the children are working through their grief the best way they know how.

Talking To Children About Death

Children are deeply affected by loss and, like adults, have a need to be heard and assisted in expressing their grief. Death is a frightening concept to many children, and parents need to explain it as simply as possible. Be straightforward and give the facts immediately. If you are not completely honest, the child may come to distrust you at a later time. It is also important, when discussing death with your children, to allow for open communication. Listen to them and let them tell you all their feelings, even the angry and ugly ones, without judgment. For everyone involved, talking is the great healer.

Try to stay away from using euphemisms such as "The baby's just sleeping for awhile," because that may give some children a fear of sleeping or of a sleeping baby. Another dangerous statement to make is "The baby's gone away." Many children will wonder if you will "go away," too.

The best concept to strive for is the truth—as simply as possible. Explain that the baby's body does not work anymore and that the baby is "dead," not "lost." (If the child thinks that the baby is "lost," he may set about trying to find it.) An approach explaining that "the baby's body does not work, so he has gone to live with Heavenly Father and Jesus" is probably best. Explain that while you're sad that the baby won't be with you for awhile, you will see the baby again someday. Emphasize that Heavenly Father didn't take the baby away, but that Heavenly Father and Jesus are taking care of the baby until you can be there to take care of it yourselves. Using the picture of "Jesus and the Children" may be a helpful tool in showing the Savior's love for children and reassuring the sibling that the baby will be happy.

Another approach in explaining death is the illustration used with many investigators in the mission field. All that is needed is your hand and a glove. The hand represents the spirit which has been sent to live in the body (the glove). When the hand is pulled out of the glove, only the body remains and the spirit goes to live with Heavenly Father and Jesus. Have the children note that without the hand in it, the glove is lifeless.

Some children feel like they have been deceived, and that there was never a baby in the first place. One mother explained that after waiting a long time to have a baby because of many complications, then finally having a stillborn daughter, her surviving daughter did not believe that there was ever a baby. This led to many feelings of anger and distrust. In this case, the parents felt it appropriate for their daughter to see and hold the baby. Many parents choose to show the surviving child pictures taken of the baby. Use your best judgment in view of your own child's special needs.

These are just suggestions and are basic frameworks; you can add to or adjust them to apply to your children and their individual needs. The most important thing is to be straight-forward and honest.

The Memorial Service

Allow your children to feel a part of the funeral arrangements and, where appropriate, to attend the memorial service or funeral. With young children (ages 3-6), use your best judgment as to whether or not it would be beneficial to have them attend.

Try to prepare your children in advance for what to expect. Be sure to explain the difference between the spirit and the body so that the actual burial will not be overly upsetting. Go through all of the elements of the funeral so there will be nothing too surprising to the children.

The funeral may be more meaningful if the child is allowed to leave something in the casket for the baby such as a picture, toy, or other special belonging. This can be a great comfort to the child and will make him feel like he is part of the occasion.

Also, try to accommodate your child's wishes even if they may not be logical. One family remembers the funeral of their baby and how their surviving daughter was fearful that the baby would be cold. They allowed their daughter to bring a blanket to put on the grave so that the baby would be warm. If gestures such as this give your child peace, don't hesitate to allow them.

Behavioral Changes

Children often have behavioral changes while grieving. These changes can include dependency, aggressive behavior, and impaired learning ability. Be patient and loving and assist the child where necessary.

There are certain specific difficulties and behaviors you may expect to see in some form or another with a grieving child:[2]

Physiological Difficulties. There may be eating and sleeping disturbances, bowel and bladder difficulties, and body distress such as stomachaches, headaches, or rashes.

Regression. Children may return to a behavior that has been given up prior to the death, such as thumb sucking, inability to tie shoes, excessive clinging to you or a favorite possession, and temper tantrums. Children of all ages regress under stress.

Fears. Normal fears may intensify. Examples: fear of the dark, of going to sleep, of going to a new place, of your leaving, or of the child himself being taken away.

Imagined guilt. Fantasies leading to guilt feelings are common. Some children are sure that they must be responsible for the death, or that they could have prevented it in some way.

Emotions. There may be periods of sadness, anger, outbursts, anxiety, crying, and boredom.

In older children, there may be problems at school such as poor grades, problems with classmates or teachers, or other signs of inappropriate behavior. Some children become rebellious as they show their anger at the world and God.

As your children demonstrate their various struggles and difficulties, try to be patient with them and give them the time and the space that they need to grieve. Be sure to welcome people outside of the family who may be able to help in some way. Other family members and friends can be a great asset at this time when you are so overwhelmed with your own grief.

Here are some additional suggestions to help your children at this difficult time:

- Pray with your child.
- Talk to your child about Heavenly Father's love.
- Have family home evening lessons on pertinent subjects such as Heavenly Father's love, being worthy to live with him again, the atonement and resurrection, the creation, etc.
- Listen to your child's comments and questions.

- Encourage your child to express emotions verbally, or by drawing, writing, actively playing, etc. Do not be alarmed if you find your preschooler play-acting the death or the funeral. This is a way young children try to understand what has taken place.
- Allow the child to participate in family rituals such as going to the cemetery—but don't force or require participation.
- Cry with your child.
- Allow the child to give the baby a gift or participate in making a memorial to the baby, even after the funeral.
- Allow the child to have a "cuddle toy," such as a stuffed animal or doll, special toy, or blanket if desired.
- Even if you are consumed by grief, try to spend time each day with the child as a reminder that you care about the living child, too.
- Try to maintain your usual schedule. This will give your child some stability in a world that has been turned upside down. Although it could be tempting, try not to send children away for extended periods of time. They need to learn to adjust—now.
- Reassure the child of your love. He or she may need more touching and holding than usual.

Remember that death intrudes on a child's typically quiet and peaceful life, taking away a certain amount of their innocence. Many children are afraid that they or another loved one may die as well. Try to lovingly address their various fears and behaviors and somehow, you will all work through this difficult time.

The baby's grandparents and siblings have special needs and desires. Grieving parents need to try to be sensitive to these needs and remember that there are others besides them who are grieving. If all generations involved in the tragedy can be mindful of one another, many unhappy feelings can be avoided. Indeed, some very special blessings can result from a sorrowful situation.

Notes

1. Margaret H. Gerner, *For Bereaved Grandparents,* (Omaha: The Centering Corp., 1990).

2. *Children's Grief,* "How to Help the Child Whose Parent Has Died." Patricia L. Papenbrock, R.N. and Robert F. Voss, M.A., Q.M.R.P., 1988, Medic Publishing Co., Redmond, Washington, p. 7.

SEVEN

Helping Those Who Grieve

Be ye all of one mind, having compassion one of another.
—1 Peter 3:8

When you are directly involved with a bereaved family, you are probably at a loss as to how to help or deal with those grieving, especially if you are grieving yourself. Whether you are very close to the family or are just an acquaintance, your attitudes and comments can have a profound effect—they can be a positive step toward healing or another source of anguish. Even though you may feel helpless and awkward, your concern, love, and willingness to help will be invaluable to the family. Following are a few suggestions for appropriate things to say and do.

Acknowledge the existence of the baby. Experts are beginning to recognize the need to treat the loss of a baby as they would the death of any other family member. To many women, even in the very early weeks of pregnancy, the loss is regarded as nothing less than the death of a child. Says one woman, "I had a miscarriage. I experienced it as the death of our child.... What helps me is to know that others view my child as real...he was real to me. The reality of conceiving this child, carrying this child, and losing this child has changed me forever."[1]

Parents need to know that you remember and care for their baby. Mention the baby's name and make the same offers to help that you would if an older child or spouse had died.

Do not be overprotective. While some of the parents' decisions may seem strange or morbid and may make you uncomfortable, encourage them to do what is right for them. Do not try to make decisions for them; they may come to resent your interference.

Do not expect parents to grieve on your timetable. One friend of a grieving couple said, "They need to get on with their lives—this isn't healthy to hold on to this grief like they have." Many parents struggle because those around them are impatient with their grief. Try to remember that grieving can take months or in some cases a couple of years before the parents feel completely ready to deal with life again. Allow parents to take all the time they need to grieve and resolve their feelings. Parents will take only the time they *need.*

Be a good listener. When the grieving parents are ready, allow them to freely express emotions without fear of judgment. When a parent grieves, some shocking and angry feelings may be expressed. Those feelings are normal and require only your acceptance, not your lecturing or opinions. Allow the parents to discuss the same things over and over if they need to; this is a good way to help them work through some difficult emotions. *Never* probe for details regarding the death of a baby.

Allow the grieving parents to cry. Crying leads to healing and can be very cathartic.

Do not disappear or avoid those who are grieving. When one woman delivered a stillborn daughter, she noticed how the people would part and let her walk through as she passed them in the hall at church. She knew they felt awkward, but to have them avoid her was an added burden. If you feel uneasy, you may find it helpful to just approach the parent, explain your feelings of awkwardness and ask how you can help. This will open the lines of communication and at least lets the parents know you care. Remember that grief is individual, and parents may handle things differently. For example, while one parent may resent your asking if she wants to hold your healthy new baby, another may find great peace in doing so. The only way to find out, however, is to ask how the parent feels, and how he or she would like you to handle certain situations.

Do not ignore the loss. While you may not avoid the grieving parents, it's possible to intensify their discomfort by pretending that nothing has happened. One man who lost a baby close to the time a family gathering was to take place was hurt when no one even made mention of his daughter. "It was as if she never existed," he explained. Many people fear upsetting the parents by mentioning the baby or their loss; but most parents appreciate being remembered, even if they do get emotional.

Remember thoughtfulness when it is most needed. The holidays or anniversary of the baby's death, birth, or due date are often very difficult times. Be especially thoughtful, caring, and patient with parents on these occasions.

Send a letter or a card. If you are uncomfortable about visiting in person, a personal note is a wonderful way to convey your feelings of love and support. If you send a card, be sure to include a brief personal note; your feelings mean more to grieving parents than a printed message. If you're uncertain about what to write, just a simple "We love you" or "Our prayers are with you" would be appreciated.

Help with practical matters. Clean the house, do yard work, tend the other children. Take a plant, dinner, or a plate of treats to the family. Many grieving parents have difficulty attending to such practical matters. Do not ask the parent, "Is there anything we can do?" Just follow your instincts, and do *something.* Although your intentions are good, by asking you put the burden back on them to ask for your help. Many parents are too proud to admit they may need help. As long as you respect the privacy of the bereaved family, your gestures will be appreciated. One woman who had a miscarriage was touched by a woman who brought over dinner one night without asking them first. "She said that she knew if she had called first, we would have declined her offer. She was right. But we sure appreciated her gesture and her caring."

Never compare tragedies. Many people have the tendency to compare the tragedy of one person with another's. Never say, "Well, I knew someone who was full-term," or "who lost a three-year old." By comparing, you are minimizing the loss of the parent; and you are also comparing things that in reality may not have much in common.

Do not philosophize. Many people feel that they have to make cliché statements and platitudes about life or philosophize as to why the baby died. Most parents know about the Lord's plan and what is expected of them, and they don't need to be reminded of doctrine or theories at this time. Knowing of gospel doctrine doesn't necessarily make the loss much easier to bear initially. Unless you have been in a similar situation and have a particular thought that was helpful to you or to a friend, do not risk putting your foot in your mouth. A simple word or card saying, "I love you," or "I'm sorry," or "I'm thinking about you" will do far more good than shallow clichés. If you are unaware of what constitutes a "shallow cliché" or any other thoughtless comment, here is a list of possible offenders:

- *"It is for the best. This is nature's way of taking care of deformities."* How could losing a baby be "for the best?" "The best" would be to have been given a healthy baby in the first place. And in many cases, as far as the parents knew, up until the time of the loss, the baby was healthy and encompassed all their dreams. Furthermore, parents do not love their baby any less because it was not perfect. Also, in many cases the cause of the loss had nothing to do with the baby, but something related to the pregnancy or within the mother's body malfunctioned. If you do not know the circumstances surrounding the loss of the baby, do not speculate.

- *"At least the baby is not suffering."* This is a hollow statement, because the baby is not alive.
- *"The baby's in a better place."* It does not matter where the baby is. The baby is not *here.*
- *"You're young, you can still have more children."* Having another baby would not replace the one that was lost. That child was an individual—a unique, special person. Also, for many people, going through another pregnancy is the last thing they want to do.
- *"At least you did not know the baby yet."* As mentioned earlier, the bond between parent and child is formed long before birth. Much of the grief comes from the fact that there was never time to create and enjoy more of those special memories that can sustain the parent through death. Again, there's never a good time to lose a child.
- *"Are you over it?"* Bereavement is not something you "get over." And you certainly never can or even want to be "over" your child's life and death.
- *"I know how you feel."* Unless you have lost a child, you do *not* know how a parent feels. And even if you have lost a child, grief is so personal that your reaction could be completely different from what someone else is experiencing. If you are sure your comment would be pertinent to the grieving parents, a more appropriate introduction to your comment would be, "I think I can relate in some way to how you feel because..."
- *"Get on with your life."* Grief *is* a part of a parent's life. The parent is experiencing some of the most poignant and significant emotions in the human experience. These emotions are an essential and normal part of life, and parents

need to experience the full spectrum of emotions involved with grief until they can enjoy happier times.

- *"It's very common,"* and *"You'll soon be pregnant again."* While both comments may be true, depending on the kind of loss and the individual woman, they imply that the loss of the baby is a minor event and easily remedied. Even worse, statements such as these suggest that the lost baby is replaceable and not a unique individual.

- *"This will give your family a reason to try harder to reach the celestial kingdom."* This statement can put pressure on families who already feel as if they cannot "measure up." Also, after such comments many families feel that they must have been so unrighteous that they needed a tragedy in order to set their priorities straight. This, in turn, makes them feel even more guilty.

- *"Count your blessings,"* and *"At least you have other children."* People who grieve *are* grateful for what they have. But again, *nothing*, including other children, can make the pain go away.

Above all, when dealing with anyone who is grieving, be patient and kind, and make some effort to show them that you care. Be sure to let the Spirit guide you when you feel unsure about a particular approach. Remember, your support and love can be a positive factor at a time when everything seems hopeless. Your compassionate influence can make a wonderful difference in others' lives.

Notes

1. Melinda Beck with Ingrid Wickelgren, Vicki Quade and Pat Wingert, "Miscarriages," *Newsweek*, August 15, 1988, p. 46

EIGHT

Spiritual Resolution: A Doctrinal Approach

And the Spirit of the Lord shall rest upon him, the spirit of wisdom and understanding, the spirit of counsel and might, the spirit of knowledge and of the fear of the Lord. —2 Nephi 21:2

After having experienced the loss of a loved one, much peace and comfort can be found within the doctrines of The Church of Jesus Christ of Latter-day Saints and its associated scriptures. While it is a common LDS belief that babies who are born alive will be resurrected and returned to their parents to be raised at another time, little has been said about those who have been lost through miscarriage, ectopic pregnancy, stillbirth, or even abortion. Spiritually, we do see the lives of these little ones "through a glass, darkly," and much of how we choose to regard these precious babies who pass so quickly through our lives must be taken on faith. However, while little has been explicitly said about these babies and their eternal fate, there are inexorable truths that can be applied to their unique circumstances.

Within the gospel, we are blessed to have the truths and knowledge of the plan of salvation to assist us through the dark and difficult times. We often hear members of the Church who have lost a loved one say, "I am so grateful for the knowledge that I will see him again. How awful to think that there is no afterlife and that this time on earth is the only chance I will have to be with him." The gospel and its principles are, indeed, the stronghold to which we cling in times of trial and tragedy.

However, while society at large does not recognize the loss of these tiny babies, what is difficult for many parents is that oftentimes members of the Church do not recognize the babies as "persons" either. And if they are not legitimate "persons," they are then considered ineligible for resurrection. Should this be true, then this time on earth *is* the only time parents will have with these little ones. Hence these lives become lost forever, and the precious benefits and comfort of the gospel and God's plan are inapplicable with regard to these babies and their grieving parents.

But man, in his limited knowledge, has made very arbitrary interpretations as to the will of God. How has it been decided that a baby who is born very prematurely but takes a breath before dying will be resurrected, when another baby, perhaps carried to term but who dies within the womb, will not? With some investigation of the principles we already hold to be true, much comfort can be found and many fears calmed about the lives of these babies who so fleetingly pass through our lives, but affect us so deeply.

The Official Stand of the Church

Statements regarding the loss of babies have only been about stillborn children. However, something can be implied about those babies who are not carried to term. In the *General Handbook of Instructions*, the following is expressed:

> The loss of a child prior to birth is an event requiring emotional and spiritual support for grieving parents. Memorial or graveside services may appropriately be held

according to the parents' needs and desires. Although temple ordinances are not performed for stillborn children, no loss of eternal blessings or family unity is implied. If desired, the family may record a name for a stillborn child on the family genealogy group record followed by the word stillborn in parentheses.[1]

Perhaps the most interesting statement regarding stillborn children is from Bruce R. McConkie in *Mormon Doctrine.* Elder McConkie states that the issues regarding these babies are

not clearly answered in the revelation so far available for the guidance of the saints in this dispensation. No doubt such things were plainly set forth in those past dispensations when more of the doctrines of salvation were known and taught than have been revealed so far to us.

That masterful document on the origin of man by the First Presidency of the Church (Joseph F. Smith, John Winder, and Anthon H. Lund) appears to bear out the concept that the eternal spirit enters the body prior to a normal birth, and therefore that stillborn children will be resurrected. It states: "The body of man enters upon its career as a tiny germ or embryo, which becomes an infant, quickened at a certain stage by the spirit whose tabernacle it is, and the child, after being born, develops into a man.". . . This interpretation is in harmony with the general knowledge we have of the mercy and justice of that Infinite Being in whose divine economy nothing is ever lost. It would appear that we can look forward with hope and anticipation for the resurrection of stillborn children.

President Brigham Young taught that "when the mother feels life come to her infant, it is the spirit entering the body preparatory to the immortal existence"; and President Joseph Fielding Smith gave it as his opinion "that these little ones will receive a resurrection and then belong to us."[2]

These statements can be particularly comforting to couples who have lost a baby, even in early pregnancy. Because of medical technology, we know the unborn baby moves and kicks very early in pregnancy, long before the woman can feel it. Brigham Young indicated that the baby's movements were a manifestation that the spirit had entered the baby's body. If this is so, then it would appear that even the tiniest of babies would be eligible for the resurrection.

The Breath of Life

The controversy surrounding babies lost through stillbirth, miscarriage, ectopic pregnancy, and abortion and their status in eternity is typically centered in the fact that these babies have never breathed *outside of the womb*. As was discussed in Chapter One, science has proven that babies breathe within the womb very early in pregnancy, but their lungs and other organs are much too underdeveloped to support them outside of the mother's body.

Much of this confusion as to what constitutes the "breath of life" can be attributed to the creation of Adam, where God "formed man of the dust of the ground, and breathed into his nostrils the breath of life; and man became a living soul." (Genesis 2:7. See also Moses 3:7.) As indicated in the scripture, Adam was not a "living soul" until God put "the breath of life" into him—he became alive at that instant. This is unlike a baby who is alive within the womb, growing and developing, for several months.

Furthermore, Elder McConkie observes that "there is a distinction between the *spirit* and the *breath of life*."[3] Abraham's account of the creation states, "And the Gods formed man from the dust of the ground, and took his spirit (that is, the man's spirit), and put it into him; and breathed into his nostrils the breath of life, and man became a living soul" (Abr. 5:7). This scripture clearly states that the act of putting the spirit and the breath into Adam were two separate actions. Therefore, in the case of the unborn, even if the breathing done within the womb does not qualify as the "breath of life," the spirit can reside within the body prior to birth, and the baby would then be considered a candidate for resurrection.

And finally, in the Doctrine and Covenants we read, "And the spirit and the body are the soul of man" (D&C 88:15). If it can be assumed that a developing baby who moves and kicks and grows has a spirit, and we know it has a body, then according to this scripture, it must have a soul. And it would be eligible for the resurrection.

The Resurrection of Every Living Thing

Elder McConkie states, "Nothing is more absolutely universal than the resurrection. Every living being will be resurrected."[4] It is interesting, too, to note how specific the scriptures are about who and what will be resurrected:

> For all old things shall pass away, and all things shall become new, even the heaven and the earth, and all the fullness thereof, both men and beasts, the fowls of the air, and the fishes of the sea;
> And not one hair, neither mote, shall be lost, for it is the workmanship of mine hand. (D&C 29:24-25)

There are no exceptions, no footnotes, no post-scripts—*everyone* will be resurrected.

The scriptures and writings of Church leaders go into great detail about all of the life forms to be resurrected. Elder McConkie states, "Animals, fowls, fishes, plants, and all forms of life were first created as distinct spirit entities in the pre-existence before they were created 'naturally upon the face of the earth.'"[5] He further states that "all forms of life occupy an assigned sphere and play an eternal role in the great plan of creation, redemption, and salvation."[6] However, Paul specified the difference between the kinds of flesh: "All flesh is not the same flesh: but there is one flesh of men, another flesh of beasts, another of fishes, and another of birds" (1 Cor. 15:39). Notice that there is no distinction made between born and unborn flesh.

The scriptures even specify how precious God's creations are to him: "Are not two sparrows sold for a farthing? and one of them shall not fall on the ground without your Father. But the very hairs of your head are all numbered. Fear ye not therefore, ye are of more value than many sparrows" (Matt. 10:29-31). Heavenly Father must have a place for these very special babies, who are surely more precious than sparrows and more noteworthy than the hairs of our heads. It is simply not in accordance with the doctrines of the Church and the scriptures for these babies to somehow disappear into a "black hole," when a sparrow, a fish, or even a plant is precious to Heavenly Father and will have a place in his kingdom.

Restoration

The concept of restoration goes hand in hand with resurrection. According to Alma, "It is requisite that all things should be restored to their proper order" (Alma 41:2). Whether this means that lost babies will be restored as fully-developed infants, or restored to their mothers' bodies to complete their development, is unclear. But comfort can be taken in the fact that they *will* be restored:

> The soul shall be restored to the body, and the body to the soul; yea, and every limb and joint shall be restored to its body; yea even a hair on the head shall not be lost; but all things shall be restored to their proper and perfect frame.
>
> (Alma 40:23)

Finally, the Prophet Joseph Smith explained that *all losses* will eventually be restored: "All your losses will be made up to you in the resurrection, provided you continue faithful. By the vision of the Almighty I have seen it" (History of the Church 5:362).

The Light of Christ

The scriptures tell us that all things are filled with the Light of Christ, which is best explained as the innate goodness that resides in each of us because of our heritage as sons and daughters of Heavenly Father. This light helps us to recognize truth and enables us to have a conscience. Simply put, it is the "Christ in all of us." The Doctrine and Covenants explains the Light of Christ and its significance:

> He that ascended up on high, as also he descended below all things, in that he comprehended all things, that he might be in all and through all things, the light of truth; Which truth shineth. This is the light of Christ.
> Which light proceedeth forth from the presence of God to fill the immensity of space—The light which is in all things, which giveth life to all things, which is the law by which all things are governed, even the power of God who sitteth upon his throne, who is in the bosom of eternity, who is in the midst of all things.
> He comprehendeth all things, and all things are before him, and all things are round about him; and he is above all things, and in all things, and is through all things, and is round about all things; and all things are by him, and of him, even God, forever and ever.... I say unto you, he hath given a law unto all things, by which they may move in their times and their seasons. (D&C 88:6-7, 12-13, 42)

If Heavenly Father is "in all things, and through all things," and "all things are by him, and of him," then it follows that these babies are special simply because they are his creations and are part of him. Perhaps these babies are merely living out the lives dictated to them because of the "law by which all things are governed." Perhaps they are living out "their times and their seasons" according to the will of our Heavenly Father.

The scriptures present a compelling argument that these babies who are lost will be resurrected. From a scriptural and doctrinal perspective, they are significant simply because they have existed on this earth. All things created by our Heavenly Father have a special status—and these much-loved babies should be no exception.

Notes

1. *General Handbook of Instructions* (Salt Lake City: The Church of Jesus Christ of Latter-day Saints, 1987), pp. 6-10.
2. Bruce R. McConkie, "Stillborn Children" in *Mormon Doctrine* (Salt Lake City: Bookcraft, 1966), p. 768.
3. Ibid., "Breath of Life," p. 105.
4. Ibid., "Resurrection," p. 638.
5. Ibid., "Spirit Bodies," p. 750.
6. Ibid., "Animals," p.38.

NINE

God Is a Loving Father

God has not ceased to be a God of miracles. —Mormon 9:15

To understand where our lost babies stand in the eternal scheme of things, it is important to understand the very nature of God and his son Jesus Christ and their divine attributes. The Lord has said, "Learn of me, and listen to my words; walk in the meekness of my spirit, and you shall have peace in me" (D&C 19:23). By understanding our Heavenly Father, perhaps we can better understand the tragedies that occur in our lives and why these things happen. The scriptures tell us,

> Believe in God; believe that he is, and that he created all things, both in heaven and in earth; believe that he has all wisdom, and all power, both in heaven and in earth; believe that man doth not comprehend all the things which the Lord can comprehend. (Mosiah 4:9)

Because many people find (quite normally) that part of the grieving process may include anger toward God, becoming reacquainted with him can be an important step in the healing process.

God Is a Loving Father

When John and Sue lost their baby because of a

miscarriage, they were plagued with the typical questions of "Why?" and "Why us?" as they struggled to understand the Lord's ways and will. John recalls that while he was driving to work one day and talking to Heavenly Father, he received an answer to their prayers. "It was as if a voice had said to me, 'I didn't want you to lose that baby, but it just has to be this way. I hurt as badly as you do." John explains that he could feel Heavenly Father's sorrow and knew he shared in their pain. "From that point on, I could learn to deal with the loss because I knew that Heavenly Father loved us and understood our pain. I could turn away from anger and blame, and concentrate on the healing process in a more positive manner."

Understanding Heavenly Father's love and accepting it can be a great help in the grieving process and can be conducive to healing. Indeed, we have his promise: "Be faithful and diligent in keeping the commandments of God, and I will encircle thee in the arms of my love" (D&C 6:20). And the apostle John reminds us that "we have known and believed the love that God hath to us. God is love; and he that dwelleth in love dwelleth in God, and God in him" (1 John 4:16). He adds that "there is no fear in love; but perfect love casteth out fear.... We love him, because he first loved us" (1 John 4:18-19). Furthermore, the scriptures specifically state that if we keep his commandments, "he will love thee, and bless thee, and multiply thee: he will also bless the fruit of thy womb" (Deuteronomy 7:13). What could be a more joyful promise to parents who have lost a little one?

God as Creator

Understanding our Heavenly Father's love is helpful in understanding his role as creator and his love for his creations. The scriptures state that he is the "great God that formed all things" (Proverbs 26:10), and that "All things were made by him; and without him was not any thing made that was made"

(John 1:3).

Knowing that *all things* are created by our Heavenly Father, including new life, is a great comfort when we understand how Heavenly Father regards his creations: "And the one being is as precious in his sight as the other. And all flesh is of the dust; and for the selfsame end hath he created them, that they should keep his commandments and glorify him forever" (Jacob 2:21). Furthermore, we can know that babies who die are not mere "mistakes," as many imply, for the scriptures also state, "He [God] is the Rock, his work is perfect" (Deuteronomy 32:4). And finally, Heavenly Father demonstrates the significance of his creations when he declares that

> all things are created and made to bear record of me, both things which are temporal, and things which are spiritual; things which are in the heavens above, and things which are on the earth, and things which are in the earth, and things which are under the earth, both above and beneath: all things bear record of me. (Moses 6:63)

God's Wisdom and Mercy

In times of tragedy and crisis, the troubled soul may be inclined to ask, "How could a loving God allow this to happen?" When Adam and Eve partook of the forbidden fruit and were cast from the Garden of Eden, they became aware of good and evil and joy and misery. The scriptures tell us that, in fact, the fall of Adam and Eve was a necessary part of God's plan. Otherwise,

> all things which were created must have remained in the same state in which they were after they were created; and they must have remained forever and had no end...wherefore they would have remained in a state of innocence, having no joy, for they knew no misery; doing no good, for they knew no sin. But behold all things have been done in

the wisdom of him who knoweth all things. (2 Nephi 2:22-
24)

While we may not know exactly why tragedies happen in
our lives and in what circumstances Heavenly Father will
intervene, we can take comfort in the knowledge that these
things happen according to God's plan; for as he said, "All
these things shall give thee experience, and shall be for thy
good" (D&C 122:7).

Similar to Adam and Eve's experience, perhaps the loss of
a baby is somehow intricately woven into a part of God's plan.
We know that mortal life is a time for us to know joy and misery, good and evil. We also know that some good can result
from the bad or the trials. In all adversity, there are lessons to
be learned which can strengthen and enhance our lives, if we
can only overcome the initial pain.

For many couples, the loss of a baby is their first experience with death and sorrow, and the fullness of joy and
thanksgiving come only after the pain is endured. Many couples speak of how much more they appreciate their children
when they realize the miracle of what it takes to get those children to earth—but enormous pain always precedes the complete joy. When we feel lost and forgotten, we can take comfort in knowing that a loving Father "looketh down upon all
the children of men; and he knows all the thoughts and
intents of the heart; for by his hand were they all created from
the beginning" (Alma 18:32).

In a situation that seems unfair and unjust, it may be difficult to concentrate on the kindness and mercy of Heavenly
Father. However, while we do not know all the reasons for our
trials, we do know that Heavenly Father wants to help us
through them. In 2 Samuel we are exhorted to "fall now into
the hand of the Lord; for his mercies are great" (2 Samuel
24:14), and in Alma we are counseled to "remember, that God

is merciful unto all who believe on his name" (Alma 32:22).

One woman who had a miscarriage explains how she understood and accepted God's mercy: "It was as if Heavenly Father said, 'I had to take your baby, but I'll help you get through it.' From that point on, I felt as if we were working on making it through together." Another woman who had a still-born daughter senses the eternal implications of her loss: "I know that Heavenly Father will return my daughter to me some day because he knows that's what needs to happen for me to be happy, and I know that God is just."

Faith

While understanding the qualities of our Heavenly Father is crucial to understanding the adversities we face, having faith in those qualities is absolutely essential to coping with the trauma of adversity. The only complication with the concept of faith is that to most of us it is just that—a concept. Exactly what does it mean to have faith in God, especially during a crisis?

The scriptures tell us in the popular verse that "faith is not to have a perfect knowledge of things; therefore if ye have faith ye hope for things which are not seen, which are true" (Alma 32:21), and also that "faith is the substance of things hoped for, the evidence of things not seen" (Hebrews 11:1). Surely this definition could apply to the lives of these little babies of whom we do not have a "perfect knowledge." Perhaps one of the purposes of their mortal lives is to teach us the meaning of faith, for "if a man knoweth a thing he hath no cause to believe, for he knoweth it" (Alma 32:18).

To survive and emerge even stronger from the tender loss of a baby, we must believe in the goodness of God, believe in his love, justice, mercy, and wisdom, and trust that all things will be resolved in a manner pleasing to him as well as to ourselves. We must believe that "the Lord is able to do all things according to his will, for the children of men, if it so be that they exercise faith in him" (1 Nephi 7:12).

When we are faced with a crisis and feel alone and forgotten, the only thing we can cling to is our belief in Heavenly Father. One woman who had a miscarriage explains, "I would just envision myself holding on to Heavenly Father's hand as I tried to make it through each day, and when things got really tough, I would just try to imagine that I could feel his loving arms around me." Indeed, it has been said, "Hold on thy way,...fear not what man can do, for God shall be with you forever and ever" (D&C 122:9).

Personal Revelation

As members of The Church of Jesus Christ of Latter-day Saints, we look with awe and wonder at the faith of the young Joseph Smith as his fervent prayer was answered and he spoke to God the Father and Jesus Christ. While visions and visitations may not be Heavenly Father's typical response to our prayers, we are told that we can receive answers, even personal revelations, if we ask. The well-known scripture which inspired Joseph Smith to pray counsels, "If any of you lack wisdom, let him ask of God, that giveth to all men liberally, and upbraideth not; and it shall be given him. But let him ask in faith, nothing wavering" (James 1:5-6).

After we have come to an understanding of our Heavenly Father and his plan for us, and have learned to develop pure faith and trust in God while keeping his commandments, we may seek answers from him regarding the losses we face—answers that perhaps only the Spirit can reveal. While the scriptures may not deal explicitly with our lost infants and the meaning of their lives, we are assured that whatever we ask in faith will be given. We are counseled to "hearken unto [him], and open your ears that ye may hear, and your hearts that ye may understand, and your minds that the mysteries of God may be unfolded to your view" (Mosiah 2:9). The Lord further promises that "whatsoever thing ye shall ask the Father in my name, which is good, in faith believing that ye shall receive, behold, it shall be done unto you" (Moroni 7:26).

One woman explains the comfort she received after many tears and prayers. After several miscarriages, Jill and her husband decided to try to have another baby. When the decision was made to risk yet another pregnancy, Jill states, "I got scared. I just felt that there was no more of me to give. I thought that if I lost another baby, I would physically die. I sat on the floor and suddenly I felt as if I was surrounded by an aura. Then, it was as if a voice spoke to me and told me we were doing the right thing, we were with the right doctor this time, and that everything would be fine. I had the most beautiful feeling, and I was finally comforted. We had to follow several precautions, but nine months later I gave birth to a beautiful little son."

Another woman explains how she found comfort while praying. "We had been trying to get pregnant, and we so desperately wanted a child. One day, feeling I could not take it any more, I poured out my heart to my Heavenly Father, when in my mind I saw a scene. I saw all of these children, and I saw a baby boy who, in my mind, I picked up. I held him close and felt a strong surge of love for him. Suddenly, I was fearful of taking him, but then was assured that it was part of God's plan. A few days later, I found out I was pregnant. We were so thrilled, but I didn't know that I would lose that baby three months later. I take comfort in that experience, though. To me it shows that my baby must have a part in God's plan, because Heavenly Father told me that he did."

Not all personal revelations are so dramatic. However, the infallible truth is that God *will* answer our prayers. Some personal revelations involve simply being touched by the Spirit through a speaker, scripture or song. Others are answers to prayer through people the Lord provides to comfort us. Still other personal revelations can be reaffirmations of the gospel and its principles and renewals of testimony. And finally, some revelations can simply be having peaceful feelings or thoughts when it seems that peace has been long forgotten. "If thou shalt ask, thou shalt receive revelation upon revelation, knowledge upon knowledge, that thou mayest know the mysteries and peaceable things—that which bringeth joy, that which bringeth life eternal" (D&C 42:61).

We can all receive the answers to calm our troubled souls in times of crisis. One woman, seeking answers to the difficult issues surrounding a stillbirth, writes about her eventual understanding:

Stillborn

Stillborn,
I am not sure that I understand.

Is it a babe who is born
In the hush of a morning's breath
Before the birds begin to sing?
No. This is not stillborn, though
We would like it to be.

Is it a babe who is born so quiet,
So still, that the angels hush
Their rustling wings to hear
If she will not draw a tiny breath?
Perhaps. This is very close, but surely,
it means more.

Stillborn,
Born, still in the arms of God.
Stillborn,
Born, still in the full knowledge of
God's love and power,

His glory and grace.

Born still to us, but alive to God!
Surely this is stillborn:
  No death, but life eternal,
  No sorrow, but everlasting peace,
  No separation, but
    communion forever
    With God!

Yes, now I understand,

Stillborn...

Linda Kay

Angel Babies

To lose a baby is surely one of the cruelest events in nature. The bond between parent and child, even yet unborn, can be one of the most profound and intimate bonds ever experienced. Losing a baby can produce a devastation so deep and so complete that many wonder if rebounding from such an experience is even possible. But the Lord has told us to "Be patient in afflictions, for thou shalt have many; but endure them, for, lo, I am with thee, even unto the end of thy days" (D&C 24:8).

Patience is not an easy thing to have during a crisis; but if we can concentrate on the love of God, allow ourselves to depend on his strength, and dedicate our lives to him, perhaps we can overcome the pain and say with the prophet Ammon, "Yea, I know that I am nothing; as to my strength I am weak; therefore I will not boast of myself, but I will boast of God, for in his strength I can do all things" (Alma 26:12).

By studying the scriptures and the writings of prophets and other Church leaders, a convincing argument can be made that our lost babies will, indeed, be resurrected.

However, perhaps the truly pertinent issue is whether or not we will be worthy to be their parents in the event of their resurrection. Joseph Smith wrote of the special nature of children who die in infancy:

> The Lord takes many away, even in infancy, that they may escape the envy of man, and the sorrows and evils of this present world; they were too pure, too lovely, to live on earth; therefore, if rightly considered, instead of mourning we have reason to rejoice as they are delivered from evil, and we shall soon have them again. (History of the Church 4:553)

This is the challenge all parents of lost babies have—to live to be worthy of such precious lives.

The way in which we allow the loss of our babies to affect our lives can decide our worthiness. We can let the loss embitter us, or we can allow the loss to serve as a springboard to greater spiritual heights, taking us closer to heaven.

Writer Ora Pate Stewart composed the following poem after the loss of her daughter, showing her determination to live worthy of having her child again:

To Glenda
Small as a jewel box is your little casket,
And you, as my smallest jewel,
Are treasured up to God within it.

I did not give you willingly,
Nor did he snatch you from me.
I rather think the choosing was your own.
Or, perhaps we three had planned together
In some other world,
That you would come and make this hasty call,
Then hurry on,

That you might light the lanterns on the way
So I could find the footing.
But I have forgotten. I think you, too,
Forgot for one brief day—
You tried so hard—
But God remembered;
And then you left me.

I took a comfort in the little clothes
I made so tenderly.
The little petticoat, the dress,
The dainty lace,
The little bonnet
That frames your tiny face.
Your eyes are closed,
And mine are dimmed with tears.
But maybe you can see with better eyes
And know I love you.

All the dreams we dreamed together,
While you were one with me—
These can wait.
I do not count them wasted.
Nor the drops of fresh warm milk
That fall unbidden from my aching breasts,
Like beads of pearl unstrung about your neck,
And caught by your fixed fingers.
These one day
Will be distilled as manna.
This milk that you never tasted
Will satiate your soul,
And life will be fulfilled.

Go then, my little jewel.
Go back to God.
Tell him I feel no bitterness at all.

With my own hands I offer you.
I have a treasure laid up in heaven.
And where my treasure lies,
My heart will follow.
You are my surety laid up with God.
And I will come to you.
I will. I will.[1]

Our lives have been compared to a tapestry that only the Lord, as the weaver, fully knows and appreciates. He sees the beautiful work from the "right" side, and we see only the tangled mess of threads on the "wrong" side. We must believe in him and trust that the intricately-woven fabric that makes up our lives is being fashioned according to his masterful design. The beauty of the fabric is in the perfect blending of the threads—some light, some dark, each one a miracle.

As we look through the "glass, darkly," we can reach up and take our Heavenly Father's outstretched hand, allowing him to walk with us through the darkness and toward the light, fearing nothing. There is no doubt that the loss of a baby can shake us to the depths of our souls. But we must remember that the loss can also take us closer to heaven. And that's where we want to be—for indeed, to lose a baby must mean that heaven needs another angel.

Notes

1. Quoted in Deanna Edwards, *Grieving: The Pain and the Promise* (American Fork, Utah: Covenant Communications, Inc., 1990), pp. 66-67.

For more information, or for assistance in dealing with the loss of unborn babies and newborns, contact your local chapter of SHARE (Source of Help in Airing and Resolving Experiences). Many chapters are listed in local telephone directories; or contact your health care provider or local hospital for information.

About the Author

Sherri Devashrayee Wittwer, a life-long resident of Salt Lake City, holds a degree in English from the University of Utah. When she lost a son through miscarriage, she began looking for Church books as a source of comfort. "To my surprise," she recalls, "there were no available books that dealt with this specific sort of grief. I desperately wanted answers, and I was sure there must be many others like my husband and me. So the idea of this book was born."

In addition to writing, Sherri's loves include reading, cooking, sports, and teaching. She and her husband, David, have two children.